RESTORE *the* TABLE

RESTORE *the* TABLE

Discovering *the* Powerful Connections of Meaningful Mealtimes

BY RYAN RUSH *with* Ken Abraham

Forefront
BOOKS

Published by Forefront Books, Nashville, Tennessee.
Distributed by Simon & Schuster.

Library of Congress Control Number: 2023922115

Print ISBN: 978-1-63763-230-7
E-book ISBN: 978-1-63763-231-4

Cover Design by Bruce Gore, Gore Studio, Inc.
Interior Design by PerfecType, Nashville, TN

DEDICATION

*This book is dedicated to the memory of my
late friend and mentor, Dr. Ralph Smith,
who shaped me, challenged me, and inspired me
over many meals together. Ralph taught me
the value of mentoring and the power of the table.*

ABOUT THE AUTHORS

About Ryan: Dr. Ryan Rush serves as the pastor of Kingsland in Katy, Texas—a thriving congregation of five thousand dedicated to bringing gospel transformation to homes. He is a graduate of the University of Mary Hardin–Baylor and Liberty Baptist Theological Seminary, and he holds a PhD in Christian leadership from Dallas Baptist University. Ryan has been married to Lana for thirty-one years, and they have three daughters. Ryan's book *Walls: Why Everybody's Stuck (and Nobody Has to Be)* was released by Tyndale House Publishers in 2011, and it shares the principles and stories of faith breakthroughs that have become an important part of church life at Kingsland.

About Ken: Ken Abraham is a *New York Times* best-selling author, known around the world for his collaborations with high-profile public figures. He has collaborated on works with Lisa Beamer, Joe Gibbs, Bill Gaither, Chuck Norris, Buzz Aldrin, and Randy Travis. Ken lives in Franklin, Tennessee, with his wife, Lisa. He's deeply invested in his family and grandchildren, a passion that drew him to this project.

CONTENTS

A PERSONAL WORD FROM RYAN

Somaliland, Africa, is often confused with its more volatile neighbor, Somalia. Somalia is the nation of *Black Hawk Down*. It's the home of the infamous pirates of *Captain Phillips* and dozens of real-life news stories. But Somaliland broke away in the 1990s through a bloody civil war, and since that time, it has been struggling to gain acceptance on the global stage and economic traction at home. Its people are proud, but in a vast wasteland of desert tundra, they have few natural resources and meager opportunities for educational advancement.

I traveled to Somaliland to help dedicate a school in one of its remote communities. It was a pleasant trip but one full of contrasts: I am a Christian, and this is a nation populated primarily by Muslims. There's not a single Christian church in the land. Still, I came away from this journey with new friends and partners. We did not convert one another on the trip, except to demonstrate the humanity of each person and cultivate an openness for an ongoing alliance. How can such a thing happen, with such vast differences in worldview, outlook, and faith? I'm convinced there was one catalyst that made all of this happen in just a few days: the meals we shared together.

My most pointed memory (besides pulling into the school courtyard full of smiling children, celebratory music, and a few camels!) was a dinner at the town hall in Gabiley, a mid-sized suburban town. There were about two dozen people present around two tables: My good friends, the McDowell family, had accompanied me from home, as the school had been dedicated in honor and memory of their late, beloved son, Will. Jerry Squyres was the liaison—a soft-spoken retired minister who now travels the world looking for forgotten places of great need. The others were leaders from the nation of Somaliland: the minister of education, the governor of that region, and the local mayor. While grateful for the new school and the hope of more to come, all of them had reason to be a bit suspicious, as we'd made no secret about our Christian faith. But what we lacked in trust in those early moments we made up for in an abundance of food on the table. There were things I could recognize: chicken with some unique, delicious red sauce and beef roast in a savory au jus. There were plenty of items that were unrecognizable. (Did I mentioned that a staple of the Somali diet is camel?) Even so, the sharing of food brought out stories around the table of family, upbringing, hopes, and dreams. Before we got up from the meal, something had changed: we had a mutual appreciation for one another, they seemed to have an interest in rather than aversion to our Christian beliefs, and we had an agreement for the next project for which we would partner in the country—a school for special needs children, which would be the first of its kind in their history and would be named for my own daughter with special needs back home.

The table changed everything.

The Challenge

I want to offer you a challenge so simple and seemingly natural that you may be surprised how life-changing it can be. This one piece of advice can improve the way you see the world, it can change your family forever, it will help your kids succeed, it will improve your relationships, and it will cost you nothing extra but time. So would you dare risk it? Would you be willing to give it a try?

This key will work. You *will* see progress. You will definitely change the lives of your family members starting today; you may even change your future family tree.

This is not some new, ethereal concept that was only recently discovered. Oddly enough, this habit has been around for all of human history, and it is not difficult to do. Quite the contrary, it is relatively easy, involving something that you may already be doing, which is why most people miss it. But once you discover the value and the simplicity of it all, the benefits will increase exponentially.

Will you accept it? Will you do it?

Of course, if I gave you an extremely difficult challenge to help your family, you'd probably do that, no matter how tough it was. If I suggested that you could accomplish such phenomenal success and that your family would prosper and be blessed by your climbing Mount Everest, walking barefoot over a bed of burning coals, running a marathon every day for a month, crawling up the Vatican steps on your knees, praying to the holy city five times a day, or cutting chocolate out of your diet, you'd probably say, "Okay, I will do that."

I'm not suggesting anything that hard. This is much easier. But perhaps in your life, it will be more radical than anything you have ever done previously.

Here you go. Are you ready to receive this? Let it impact you, wash over you, and sink into your heart, mind, spirit, and will.

This is the "secret": *Have five meaningful mealtimes with people you love each week and share one of those same meals once a month with someone outside your normal circle.*

You don't even have to cook those meals; they can consist of take-out burgers or frozen dinners. They can be around kitchen tables or picnic tables. They just have to be meals you're already experiencing that you choose to share intentionally with others.

"What! That's all?" I hear you saying. "You've got to be kidding!"

That's it. Five meaningful meals together with the people you love can be the difference-maker between families that thrive and those that barely survive.

I hear you saying, "Anybody can do that."

Yes, anybody can. *But most people don't.*

You may have noticed that the number of families that have regular mealtimes together is in decline. Some estimates say that in the past twenty years, the frequency of family dinners has dropped 33 percent. The *Atlantic* reported that "the average American eats one in every five meals in the car, one in four Americans eats at least one fast food meal every single day, and the majority of American families report eating a single meal together less than five days a week."[1] Even beyond family time, we're simply finding ourselves alone more often. A recent study featured in *Nutrition* demonstrated that people who ate alone demonstrated significantly less healthy eating habits.[2] Even beyond mealtimes, our social worlds are more fractured than ever. A recent NPR report revealed this to be most pronounced among young adults ages fifteen to twenty-four who experience 70 percent less interaction with others as opposed to the norms two decades ago.[3]

Think about it. When was the last time you had a sit-down meal with people you care about that lasted longer than thirty minutes? With the television off and the absence of music, phones, or other distractions?

Was it really last week that you had a meaningful meal with your family? Or last month? Or was it so long ago you cannot remember? You are not alone. Many families in America are struggling to find time to sit down and have a meal together.

A number of factors have contributed to the decline in families eating together. Obviously, employment outside the home, traffic congestion, and longer work hours all make gathering for supper a more strategic operation, if it is done at all. Extracurricular school activities and even church functions can vie for family members' time in such a way as to make mealtimes together rare or, at best, quick and perfunctory.

All the while, studies continue to contend that mealtimes together as a family matter—and they matter a lot! According to the American Psychological Association's 105th annual convention, well-adjusted teens (meaning they are less likely to abuse drugs, less likely to be depressed, more motivated at school, and have better peer relationships) eat with their families an average of five days per week.[4] One study published in the *Journal of Adolescence* revealed that frequent (five or more) family meals brought about more positive family relationships, higher well-being, lower depression, and fewer risk-taking behaviors. Interestingly, these results held true regardless of the housthold's income, cultural background, or even parenting style.[5]

Another study published in the *Journal of Adolescence* demonstrated the importance of adding meaning to those mealtimes. By surveying five hundred households that conducted regular family mealtimes, those who had intentional engagement between parents and children during those meals also had children who demonstrated significantly better emotional well-being.[6]

This is not a new concept. We know that it is often easier to form friendships and deeper relationships when we share a meal together. Businesspeople frequently find it easier to negotiate deals over meals than in an office. And everyone knows the value of going out to dinner or having coffee when it comes to establishing a dating relationship. Something about having a meal or a drink together draws us closer to one another.

I'm the Senior Pastor of Kingsland Baptist Church, a large, thriving congregation in Katy, Texas, about a thirty-minute drive from downtown Houston when traffic is moving and Interstate 10 is not serving as a parking lot. In our church, we have some of the best people in all the world: bright, ambitious, talented people who love God, love their families, and love other people—people who want the best for their families and who want to influence the world positively. As you might imagine, I've learned much from our congregation. I've also studied the Bible for years, and I have discovered some fascinating information about God, people, life, and eternity. I earned a PhD by investigating the impact parents have on the future leaders they are raising, and I found consistent evidence of a connection between the two. *Forbes* magazine estimates that the corporate world invests $366 billion per year in leader development, but evidence demonstrates that the most influential leadership development happens long before most realize: every time moms and dads are investing in their children.[7] How we lead as adults, how we follow others in authority around us, and how we were raised are tightly linked. In fact, I found that such connections are not limited by cultural boundaries; my studies, and the significant results connecting parenting and leadership, extended across four continents. Such influence involves the earliest feelings of safety and security the child feels in the presence of his caregivers through the most basic activities of conversation, correction, quality time, and, of course, mealtimes.

But I have also discovered that you don't need to be a religious person, a Bible scholar, an engineer, or the possessor of several university degrees to know that mealtimes matter more than we imagine—and not merely for physical nourishment! Our past mealtimes have influenced our present, and our future mealtimes will positively or negatively affect the people we love.

So I presented a challenge to our congregation. "Moms and dads, grandparents, do you know what your kids need more than great schools and good tutoring and the right sports league and that great vacation you are considering? They need to share a meal with you on a regular basis. They need to catch who you are and experience life with you when it is not a special occasion." I continued by giving some specific suggestions for how we could reclaim our dining tables.

"Can we choose to have five meaningful mealtimes each week with the people we love?" I asked.

Hundreds of people agreed to experiment with the concept, and the results were astounding. Our people reported news that seemed almost too good to be true: marriages were strengthened, moms and dads were less stressed, siblings were calmer and got along better, people who had been fighting addictions for years began to face those challenges head-on, and in more than a few cases, students' academic grades improved. Families were profoundly affected by doing this one simple thing: having five meaningful mealtimes together each week. They realized that if they could capture this one thing, surely other good things would happen in their family as well. And they did.

An Added Challenge

When the COVID pandemic shut down the world in 2020, we experienced a social separation unlike anything most of us have experienced in our lifetimes. Not only were we physically separated for long periods of time but the social and political hot topics of that season seemed to divide people even further.

The pandemic provided a new opportunity for the members of our church: suddenly, five meaningful mealtimes with the people in our households was almost automatic because so many people were stuck at home. Then, as the world opened up a bit, we offered a new opportunity: What if, on top of our five meaningful mealtimes, we used those same principles to invite someone to the table who might normally be outside our comfort zones? Given the circumstances and settings of the pandemic, this was mostly a challenge to connect with our closest neighbors.

You may wonder whether eating with a neighbor is *really* that far out of anyone's comfort zone, but in West Houston, we have a unique demographic: Kingsland is located in Katy, Texas, one of the most ethnically diverse communities in America. Transplanted people come from all around the world because of the oil industry in Houston. Walking through almost any grocery store in Katy, it will appear as though the United Nations is having a conference in town. Some people are dressed in stylish, exquisite suits, other people wear burkas, still others look as though they have just come out of an ancient Chinese temple. More than ninety separate languages are spoken in Katy. Indeed, our fastest-growing ministry at Kingsland is our Mandarin ministry.

This cultural diversity adds a wonderful flair to everyday life in our community. We host our annual International Festival to celebrate that very thing. Even so, those cultural backgrounds create unavoidable barriers because of the differences in language, faith, politics, and worldviews. One thing we found that all of us appreciate, however, is food. And sharing our favorites from "back home" turns out to be a great way to build bridges with neighbors. Borrowing the theme "Love Where You Live" from a grassroots campaign a few years earlier in Austin, Texas, several churches in our region joined together in this challenge to share time with our neighbors. Once again, we heard some amazing stories of something as simple as a shared meal bringing down walls between people who had otherwise been worlds apart. Conversations started and friendships were born. As all of this played out, I realized the power of adding the monthly "comfort zone" challenge to the five family mealtimes that we had found so impactful previously.

At Kingsland, we are not bashful about saying that our goal is to see 1,000,007 homes transformed by Jesus.

It may seem odd to include that seven, but we want to remember that we won't impact a million if each of us doesn't seek to influence seven homes by letting them know God loves them. I've spoken with leaders from all over our community who have similar dreams: to see their neighbors experience the joy and peace that they have known. I'm convinced that the meals challenge is a simple step toward seeing these dreams fulfilled. As families come together on a regular basis and welcome others to the table, good things are bound to happen. How can they not? When people purposely share meals together, matters of spiritual importance with eternal value can occur naturally too.

Understand, five meaningful mealtimes does not mean merely snatching a grab-and-go breakfast in the morning as you head out the door. Nor does it mean eating dinner while watching television, or scarfing down some food while you or your family members are talking on phones, or surfing the Internet, or sharing texts or calls with someone else throughout the meal.

In the pages ahead, we'll explore what we mean by five meaningful mealtimes each week with the people you love, why they are important, and how you can incorporate them into your busy lifestyle. You will also find some stories of people whose lives were transformed forever by meaningful mealtimes. Get ready—your life is about to change for the better!

CHAPTER 1

Jesus's Table

Jesus seemed to especially enjoy eating with people and talking with them about spiritual truths over meals. He often visited in the home of His friends Lazarus, Mary, and Martha, sharing meals and conversation.

He was also willing to eat with people the religious folks shunned and avoided. For instance, it must have really stunned people in Jericho when Jesus spotted the chief tax collector, Zacchaeus—a known shyster— perched in a tree watching the parade of people pressing around Jesus as He passed by. In the middle of that crowd, Jesus looked at Zacchaeus, and said, "Zacchaeus, hurry and come down, for today I must stay at your house."[8] Everybody in town knew that Zacchaeus was a sinner, and so did Jesus, but He still went to the tax collector's home for a meal, and Zacchaeus's life was changed for the better.

It shouldn't come as a surprise to see Jesus constantly around the table. He was, after all, of Hebrew descent, and all of the traditional Jewish festivals involved food. In fact, they were known as the seven *feasts* of Israel. Luke 2 reminds us that Mary and Joseph followed these festivals faithfully, so undoubtedly, Jesus had many unforgettable moments around the table as He grew up.

Early in His public ministry, when Jesus called Matthew, another well-known tax collector, to follow Him, the first place they went was to Matthew's house for a meal with all of Matthew's pagan friends.[9] Clearly, Jesus knew that people tended to relax more over food, that their minds and hearts were often more open to truth and new ideas as they ate together.

The night before Jesus faced His death on the cross, He hosted a special Passover meal for His closest disciples. Stop and think about that for a moment. Don't rush past the significance of Jesus's choice. He could easily have called a "special, high-level meeting" with His disciples in a private boat on the Sea of Galilee. Or He could have sequestered them somewhere in a secret room in the temple in Jerusalem. But He didn't do that.

On the night before Jesus was crucified, when He was aware that His earthly ministry was coming to a close, that last gathering together with His disciples took on incredible importance. How could the Lord get across the step He was about to take, the plan that was in place, and the way forward to these men whose worlds were about to be turned upside down?

A meal. They would celebrate the Passover together one last time.

The Passover wasn't just any meal, of course. It was a symbol put in place generations earlier so households would remember the goodness and mercy of God. But Jesus didn't merely use the mealtime to communicate a timeless message; Jesus used the mealtime to communicate that, in a sense, He was giving Himself to do for them what meals had done: bring them together from that point forward. He gave them a way to demonstrate their ongoing faith by taking in the bread and the wine.

Even after Jesus rose from the dead, gathering together with His disciples for meaningful mealtimes was important to Him. At least two of His post-resurrection appearances occurred when food was involved: First, at the dinner table with the disciples after walking with two of them on the road to Emmaus, near Jerusalem.[10] Then several weeks after the crucifixion and resurrection, Jesus prepared breakfast for His disciples on the shore of the Sea of Galilee, where He both instructed Peter to feed His sheep and prophesied how Peter would die.[11]

In one of the most climactic pictures of things yet to come, Jesus is revealed at the marriage supper of the Lamb and proclaimed King of kings and Lord of lords.[12] So all through the Bible, from the beginning of history to the end, meaningful mealtimes matter. Physical food can connect people and prepare them to receive spiritual food.

"So what?" you may be asking. "Why does that matter to me?"

Simply this: If the people of God and the Son of God found that meaningful mealtimes together improved relationships, maybe having five meaningful mealtimes each week with your family may prove significant as well. Christ's example also has relevance for anyone who might live alone. It's noteworthy that Jesus never married or had children, but He saw meaningful mealtimes as a significant way to cultivate lasting relationships.

Why do mealtimes matter so much? Because they mattered to Jesus.

What "Breaking Bread" Actually Means

The Hebrew word for bread is "לֶחֶם"—loosely pronounced "lekh'-em." It is a word that can be used to mean either "bread," "food," or "flesh." It implies that the breaking of bread is "sharing flesh," sharing life together. In a real way, that is what the Christian sacrament of Communion is all about. It is not merely sharing some bread and wine, crackers or grape juice. It is about sharing *life* together and connecting with one another on a spiritual level.

Throughout Scripture, food is often associated with identification and with connection. To ingest food was to proclaim, "I am connected with this concept. I believe in this idea." That is basically what Christians are saying when we take part in Communion, celebrating the Lord's Supper. The food symbolically represents Christ's broken body and His blood, and when we partake of it, we are identifying with Jesus, remembering His sacrificial death for us, and connecting with others in the family of God.

Moreover, food is often portrayed in the Bible as a symbol of our dependence on and our fulfillment in the Lord. That's why Jesus responded to the devil the way He did, when the Enemy tried to tempt Him to turn stones into bread after He had been in the wilderness for forty days without food. Jesus reminded the devil of Scripture, saying, "It is written, 'Man shall not live on bread alone, but on every word that proceeds out of the mouth of God.'"[13]

What was that all about? Simply this: Jesus was declaring afresh that our greatest need is not for physical food but for spiritual food.

Another important spiritual aspect of food, besides mere physical nourishment, is the fellowship factor. Throughout Scripture, where there is food, there is fellowship, genuine *koinonia*, real communion. In the early church, the first Christians frequently gathered together around a meal. "And day by day, attending the temple together and breaking break in their homes, they received their food with glad and generous hearts, praising God and having favor with all the people. And the Lord added to their number day by day those who were being saved."[14] Clearly, food played a key role in their fellowship.

Having a meal together unites people like nothing else can. Regardless of culture or ethnic backgrounds, gathering around the table and sharing food together can be a tremendous unifier. It is still true today: where there is food, there is fellowship!

CHAPTER 2

The Table Defines You

Regardless of your upbringing, the mealtimes around your family table have had a profound influence on your life, whether you realize it or not. Everything from your sense of personal worth and security to your concepts of God probably can be traced back to your family mealtimes, or lack of them.

My own concepts about what matters in life were largely shaped around our family tables. I don't have many memories of my maternal grandmother, but I do recall that she loved to cook—and I sure enjoyed eating Grandma Morgan's delicious food! Grandpa Morgan was in the military, so after World War II, Grandma, Grandpa, and Mom (an only child) lived in Japan as well as various places in France, Germany, and parts of Africa. Everywhere they moved, Grandma found fantastic recipes, brought them home, and passed them on to her family members, including my mom, who attended high school in Ethiopia. Food preparation and presentation became especially important to her, so I became the beneficiary of some fabulous family meals.

When it came time for my grandfather to retire from the army, Grandma Morgan was dealing with the beginnings of what would become debilitating arthritis. They found the treatment she needed at a military hospital in Alabama. Realizing the importance of remaining nearby her doctors, Grandpa and Grandma Morgan chose to live alongside the shores of Lake Martin, Alabama. My mom's family had lived in spectacular places all over the world, but by this time, their highest priority was to be away from the hustle of life and, in some ways, "off the grid." They purchased a double-wide trailer and modified it by building onto it. For the first few years in that lakeside retreat, they didn't even have a phone! The decor was an eclectic amalgamation of items they had purchased over the years from all around the world. They had exotic animals from Africa stuffed and hung on the wall, along with rare art from Japan, a bronze table from the Middle East, and a zebra skin rug on the floor. The smell of my grandfather's pipe smoke perpetually wafted through the air. Like so many grizzled war veterans, Grandpa was a heavy drinker. His mahogany bar was the centerpiece of his living room—and it seemed, at times, his life. In his best moments, however, there were few more thoughtful and insightful men to spend time with. During his moodier moments when the drinks were flowing, my grandmother was the calming presence who brought light back into the darkness. Grandma's love and food always smoothed things over. In fact, both Grandma *and* Grandpa were skilled in the kitchen—and eating at their home was often a cultural experience.

Grandma Morgan's Chinese Almond Chicken

Ingredients:

1 3/4 cups boneless chicken cut in 1/4 inch cubes (1 pound)

2 tbsp peanut or salad oil

1 cup bamboo shoots cut in 1/4 inch cubes

3/4 cup canned button mushrooms cut in 1/4 inch cubes

3/4 cup water chestnuts, cut in 1/4 inch cubes

2/3 cup dishcloth gourd or cucumber

1 1/2 cups water or mushroom liqueur

1 1/2 tbsp water

1 1/4 cup blanched almonds, chopped fine

2 or 3 green onions, chopped fine

1/2 tbsp fresh or dried ginger root

1 tsp sugar

1 1/3 tbsp soya

1 tsp salt

1 1/2 tbsp cornstarch

Instructions:

1. Peel and mash the ginger; add the soya and sugar.
2. After 5 minutes, squeeze out as much liquid as possible and discard the ginger.
3. Mix this liquid with the chicken.
4. Chop the almonds very fine.
5. Heat 1 tbsp oil in a frying pan and fry the almonds until they are a delicate brown.
6. Remove from fire and add 1/2 tsp table salt.
7. Heat 1 tbsp oil until it is very hot.
8. Fry the chicken in it for 4 to 5 minutes.
9. Add the bamboo shoots, mushrooms, cucumbers, green onions, water chestnuts, salt, and 1 1/2 cups of water or mushroom liqueur.
10. Simmer for 3/4 hour or until the chicken is tender.
11. Mix cornstarch and 1 1/2 tbsp water to form a smooth paste. Pour it into the chicken mixture and simmer for 5 minutes, stirring constantly.
12. Just before serving, add 1 cup of the almonds.
13. Place in a serving dish and sprinkle the remaining 1/4 cup of almonds on top.

At dinner, we sat around a central dining table, enjoying Grandma's French dishes such as steak tartare or tasty Japanese stir-fry with fresh vegetables done in a wok. And then there were her sensational homemade desserts. All of those things took time to prepare, but it was never wasted time. There was love and laughter in the kitchen and conversation leading up to the meal itself. After the meal came rest, relaxation, and more conversation. Grandma and Grandpa's table was a unifying factor for our family, and we shared lots of joy around the dining table.

More than the marvelous smell and taste of the food, though, the experience of gathering around the table as a family was foundational to me, listening to and participating in conversations that mattered to my parents and grandparents. Every entrée came with a story from its origin: where Grandma and Grandpa first discovered it, who was around the table, and funny stories that ensued. I treasure those early memories of meals with my grandparents.

They often unwittingly spoke words of love and encouragement, sometimes words of challenge or correction, never preaching, but merely talking in casual ways about the events of the day in a context of timeless truths and old stories. For instance, Grandpa was serving in Little Rock, Arkansas, during the height of the integration battles of the early 1960s. President Eisenhower had federalized the National Guard in 1957 and sent one thousand paratroopers in to enforce the laws. When my grandfather arrived a few years later, things were hardly settled down. Grandpa was ready and willing to step into the fray. He was one of the highest-ranking officers to volunteer his assistance in ensuring the safety of students. While the details are fuzzy today, I can still remember the pride in knowing I was part of a household that stood for what was right in the face of widespread opposition. In subtle ways, I learned the values of my family. We discovered a common bond at the table. Having those meals together connected us as a family, despite Grandpa's heavy drinking.

Grandma Morgan passed along to my mom numerous encouragements for meaningful mealtimes. A few years ago, my mom gave my wife, Lana, and me a book of memories and meals in which she shared some of those secrets. Here are just a few:

- *Presentation is more important than tastes*
- *The key to a great party is making your guests feel special.*
- *Don't get stressed out if something burns or doesn't turn out as you expected; just smile and order pizza!*

In my earlier years, my dad seemed to be working all the time, so we didn't often eat together as a family. He was not only a pilot in the air force but a highly respected veteran of Vietnam and recipient of the prestigious Silver Star. The air force carried our family to several places in my preschool years: from Mississippi to Canada to

South Carolina, and finally, to Austin, Texas, where Dad stepped into civilian life. All of these stops meant even more new experiences and memories around tables with family and friends.

After the military, Dad helped start a regional airline, which became the first of many adventures.

My father had grown up on an Indiana farm and had inherited a relentless work ethic as well as an innate ability to cultivate ideas into reality. Like corn from seeds in the ground, I witnessed so many times where Dad would begin with very little and grow a business into something of substance.

When we traveled to Indiana to be with Dad's family, life likewise revolved around food, but in this case, the relationship began much *earlier* in the process, when vegetables were still in the ground and meat was still out to pasture. I have wonderful memories of harvesting corn with my cousins and enjoying the spoils of the harvest. I recall huge spreads on the table at the old farmhouse where Uncle Steve and Aunt Carol lived (and for that matter, the same farmhouse where Aunt Carol was *born!*). In the midst of the laughter and antics of a dozen cousins with the older generations, you could sense a strong bond to the past and an appreciation for God's provision.

My dad's farm heritage was impressive and no doubt led to his ability to outwork almost anyone else I knew.

Of course, that same work ethic also took time and energy that often left him toiling long hours and away from many family mealtimes. Dad had a heart attack when I was in the sixth grade, and it seemed to serve as an alarm that caused him to dramatically adjust his lifestyle and his schedule. My father's own father had died in his midforties, so the heart episode was a wake-up call for Dad. About that same time, while we had been raised in church, my sister and I went to summer camp with a church group where, for the first time, we both fully understood the foundational truths we'd been taught. We understood, for instance, that we could have a personal relationship with Jesus, and we became Christians. This not only began a fresh journey for us kids but also seemed to stoke the fires of our parents' faith. Between that transforming change and the new awareness that Dad was not bulletproof, things began to slow down. Our family met around the dinner table much more regularly.

Moreover, my mom and dad enjoyed having friends in for meals at our home. It was not unusual for overnight guests, such as visiting revival speakers from our church or Dad's fellow aviation buffs, to stay in our home, and the mealtime conversations were an education in themselves. Mom loved to cook, so to have more people around the table who enjoyed her food was a happy place for her. Mom and Dad welcomed my sister's and my friends to eat with us, too, sometimes three or four friends at a time or more. As chaotic as it could be, our parents were always open to having my friends—a bunch of teenage boys—eat with us. It was chaotic. My friends were big, rowdy, athletic boys who consumed high volumes of food, so Mom was on a perpetual quest, constantly searching for deals on large portions of food, long before the big boxstores became popular.

Many of my meals during that time took place in the kitchen rather than in the dining room. I grew up in the 1970s and 1980s, so our kitchen was replete with bright yellow, green, and orange colors; matching wallpaper; Formica countertops; multicolored plates; and green, beveled tea glasses.

Mom's traditional Christmas dinner took on a distinctly British tone, including prime rib, Yorkshire pudding, and a trifle pudding for dessert. My parents took special efforts to make sure that nobody we knew would eat Christmas or Thanksgiving dinner alone. There was always more room at our table, especially for a person who had nowhere else to go for the holidays. There were many who joined us who were down on their luck. Others came to our table after being rejected from other tables. I think about an African American military officer and his family when both of our families were stationed in Sumter, South Carolina. It was the 1970s and the impact of segregation was still very present in the culture. They had a son my age, so I was especially thrilled to have them join us for dinners and for some good playtime afterward. Throughout my childhood, my parents were quick to invite people to join us around the dinner table. "You are welcome here" were words I heard Mom or Dad say frequently to family, friends, and sometimes even to total strangers.

I knew, long before I ever became a Christian, the power of mealtimes to connect people. The sights, sounds, smells, and tastes of good food can draw people together like nothing else can. It is true in every culture throughout history, and it is still true today.

Foods That Leave a Bad Taste in Your Mouth

Most of my memories of family mealtimes are sources of great joy. But a few of my own experiences make me wish I could have a do-over. For instance, when my wife, Lana, and I were newly married, she made some sloppy joes for us to eat. Lana's sandwich tasted okay but not as delicious as ones made by my mom, so in my naive, newlywed insensitivity, I tried to help Lana by asking, "Hon, what recipe are you using for these sloppy joes?"

"Oh, Ryan, there is no real recipe for sloppy joes," Lana said. "You can just go to the grocery store and buy a package of Manwich or something, add that to the ground up hamburger, and you are all set. There's not really a recipe."

"Darlin', there is a recipe, actually," I responded. "You know, you should call my mom. Mom makes a *great* sloppy joe. I'm sure if you asked her, she'd be glad to share the recipe with you."

Ouch! Lana's countenance changed instantly.

"Thanks," she said frostily. Although she didn't say it aloud, her expression said, "Why don't you get your mom to make you some sloppy joes!"

Lana was determined to show me my ignorance regarding the ingredients in delicious sloppy joe sandwiches, so she called my mother and asked her, "What can of seasonings do you use in your sloppy joe mix?"

"Oh, Lana, it doesn't come out of a can," my mom told her. "It's not complicated; in fact, it is a simple recipe, but there are some essential ingredients that must be included if you want the sandwiches to taste good." My mom shared the recipe with Lana.

The next time Lana made sloppy joes, she used the ingredients suggested by my mom. "Oh, wow," she said after tasting the sandwich. "This is better!"

"Mmm," I agreed.

The "Sloppy Joe Affair" was a silly incident that Lana and I still laugh about to this day. It also provides Lana a good illustration to share with newlywed husbands how *not* to communicate with their spouses. And yes, this story still comes up often on nights when sloppy joes are on the menu.

My Mom's Sloppy Joe Recipe

Ingredients:

1 pound ground beef

1/4 cup diced onion

1 cup ketchup

1 tbsp yellow mustard

1 tbsp Worcestershire sauce

1 tbsp white vinegar

1/2 tsp celery seed

Instructions:

1. Brown the hamburger meat with the onions
2. Drain and return to pan
3. Add the rest of the ingredients
4. Stir and heat it through
5. Taste, and add more of anything to your liking
6. Enjoy!

Memories of certain foods can cause us to respond physically and emotionally.

Lana and I are parents to three beautiful daughters. Our youngest daughter, Lily, was born with special needs and multiple health issues, so Lana and I spent the first hundred days of Lily's life in various hospitals with her. We got used to having a travel bag ready to go, and we became quite familiar with hospital cafeteria food. There were few restaurants that delivered to our nearest hospital at that time, but one that did was Jason's Deli. Lana and I grew to know their menu well.

Jason's Deli offered what they called a "Nutty Mixed Up Salad," a delicious salad with goat cheese, nuts, and apple slices, topped with raspberry vinaigrette dressing. We ordered that salad frequently. Well-intentioned friends and family members who visited us in the hospital learned that we enjoyed that particular salad, so they kindly brought salads for us. Bunches of them! We ate so many Nutty Mixed Up Salads that we got sick of them.

By the time we finally took Lily home from the hospital, neither Lana nor I wanted to see another Nutty Mixed Up Salad ever again. To this day, that tasty salad reminds us of pain. It tastes like hurt and disappointment.

While some foods will always have a bad memory attached to them, others can be redeemed with a slight perspective shift. When Lana started seeing one of our family's favorite desserts in a different light, it put a marvelous taste back in our mouths.

Rather than me telling you about it, Lana wrote about the change in a blog, so I'll let her tell you in her own words about the transformation that took place.

LANA'S BLOG:

The Goodbye Dessert

Recently, as I was making one of our family's favorite desserts, I had a revelation. I suddenly realized that this particular delicious treat had become our "goodbye dessert."

Certain foods evoke special memories for me. Chicken and dumplings, for example, remind me of my Mamaw. Prime rib and popovers remind me of my first Christmas with my in-laws, when I was appalled that they were not having ham, as my family had always done in Texas. Bruschetta reminds me of a family trip to Italy and a meal at a delightful, tucked-away restaurant. Breakfast pizza reminds me of Christmas morning.

While telling friends and family about our upcoming, completely unexpected, and out-of-the-blue move from Austin to Katy, Texas, I attempted to sweeten the news with a little dessert. I hoped that blueberry crisp, with a burst of warm crust and fresh blueberries covered in ice cream, with a delectable maple topping, might soften the blow just a little bit.

I'm not at all sure that my plan worked, not even for me.

I distinctly remember reaching for Kleenex facial tissue rather than my bowl of melting ice cream over blueberries, the mixture slowly turning purple.

Maybe that's why I rarely made this dessert after that. My heart started to ache every time I thought about making it, because I associated it with goodbyes. But it's just too good of a dessert to have a sad memory tied to it.

So I made it this past Monday night and shared it with my parents.

And no one said a word about goodbyes.

As I scraped my bowl clean, I had another revelation. (*Side note here—I am perfectly agreeable to getting revelations through the eating of dessert!*) This doesn't need to be a "goodbye" dessert. In fact, it could just be a friendly dessert, something to serve for any occasion. A warm and sweet way to say goodbye, or hello, or welcome to the neighborhood, or congratulations, or happy birthday, or you get the idea. Best of all, it could be a regular-old-night-of-the-week-hanging-out-with-the-family kind of dessert.

So goodbye, sad little dessert.

Say hello to the new, *happy* little dessert.

Here's the recipe for the best blueberry crisp you've ever tasted.

Ingredients:

4 cups of blueberries
1 cup of old fashioned oats
1/2 cup of pecans (or walnuts)

1/2 cup of almond meal (or 1/4 cup almond meal and 1/4 cup
   unsweetened coconut flakes)
1/4 cup of maple syrup
1/4 cup of olive oil

Instructions:

1. Pour the berries into a baking dish. In a separate bowl, mix
   the remaining ingredients using a fork, then pour the mixture over the berries.
2. Bake at 350 degrees for 30 to 40 minutes, or until just a little brown. If you're waiting for a deep, rich brown, you'll be
   waiting forever, so just pull it out of the oven when the fruit is
   bubbling and there is a little golden color on the crisp.

(Adapted from the cookbook *Bread and Wine* by Shauna Niequist)

What did Lana do? She turned that negative memory
into a positive experience that our family continues to
enjoy. You can do something similar with some of your
negative tastes.

For some people, though, similar reminiscences
evoke deep pain because their lives have been defined
more negatively by their previous family mealtimes.
Perhaps there was anger or abuse or hurtful comments
expressed around the table. Those things can leave lasting impressions in our hearts and minds.

Drawing Your Family Table

For years, at various conferences, seminars, and retreats, I have handed out blank sheets of paper and asked people to draw a picture. "Draw how you remember your family table as a child," I ask.

The responses to this simple exercise are profound. Some draw happy stick-figure faces around a table; others draw sad or angry faces; some leave empty chairs where a dad or a mom is missing. I can recall one young lady who was the daughter of a pastor drawing a picture of her family eating dinner on one side of the page and her father on the other side of the page in an easy chair watching television. Even then, before I had kids, I remember thinking that I never wanted such a family portrait in my future! I can recall another picture in which an older gentleman drew a hot-air balloon with his "stick-figure father" in the basket. On the other side of the page, he drew his family around the table eating dinner, but he was looking back at his dad as he floated away. He stated that his father was always distant, and no matter how hard he tried, he could never reach him.

We all seem to have some long-lasting memories of our tables, and the impact of those memories can be significant. Whether you realize it or not, your own table experience creates emotional pictures in your mind that will define you.

Our Attachments to the Table

Attachment science has been a major part of my research of families in recent years. Attachment science studies the strong emotional connections we inherently desire to have with our parents or caregivers—and later in life with those closest to us. The level to which we develop secure attachments early in life will often have a major impact on all other relationships later on.

British psychologist John Bowlby began investigating the well-being of children in the 1940s, focusing first on the positive aspects of the relationship children had with their mothers.[15] Building on these concepts, he demonstrated that every person has a deep, hardwired sense of need for emotional connection with others, and the strength of those earliest connections will help determine patterns from then on. The child evaluates the security of attachment relationship based on the parents' response to cries for help and their readiness to be available when needed.

As attachment theory has grown more robust through extensive research, evidence continues to reinforce the foundation of the theory: infant-caretaker relationships were significantly influential in shaping how individuals dealt with broader relationships throughout life. These *internal working models* cause us to make unconscious decisions about how we connect with people and whether to trust them.

This holds true for more than later family relationships, by the way. Researchers discovered that how you attached to mom or to dad profoundly influences how you relate to other children in grade school, how you relate to teachers, how you deal with a spouse, and how you accept leadership and authority. It all comes back to a foundational question every child asks: Can I trust my mom and dad to care for me?

Interestingly, the health of our relational attachment is rooted in perceptions of love and security from caregivers stemming from our early memories. These perceptions are based on consistent interactions over time. The dinner table can play a significant role in cultivating such connections. Meaningful mealtimes can impact every single relationship for the rest of a child's life. Think of some of the ways a child's security can be enhanced simply by having regular meals with mom and dad: physical proximity, eye contact, physical touch, and contentment all reinforce the love of the caregiver. The reinforcement of care that children receive at the table can be significant even with foster children or adopted children who have no blood relationship to the family.[16]

Given how significantly our earliest relationships impact the way we relate to others throughout life, the dinner table becomes all the more significant. In a sense, every time a child gathers with his or her parents around a meal, that child is being told, "You are important to us, and your needs will be met." Conversely, when such basic needs (for both food and the socialization of eating together) are removed, there are significant consequences.

For years, experts have only theorized that what happens around the family table has long-term effects on us. Research now, however, has consistently shown that such impact is not merely anecdotal; it has been clinically proven. It is substantive; now we know that our kids can be profoundly influenced by the early attachments made around the family table—or not made.

Something important takes place when we sit together around the table. It is at the table that each child comes to understand that even though he or she is different, each person is special. The positive results are that family life becomes social, special, spiritual, faithful, and meaningful.

Where do you start individually?

Begin by looking at the tables where you formerly sat when you were a child. Think through what you experienced there, consider how those mealtimes influenced you, and understand that in many ways, you are a product of those tables.

Years ago when bestselling author John Trent was serving as a youth pastor, he and his wife, Cindy, didn't have much money, so they bought an unfinished wooden table that they worked on together and finished themselves. Throughout the early years of their marriage, they shared many meals and conversations around that table. It is still in their family today as they have passed it down to their children.

In a similar way, the tables in your past have shaped you. You are a product of those tables that you sat around in your childhood. Go back and look at those and see if you can discover what they say about you. Were those good times in your life or hurtful times? Did you feel accepted and valued, or insignificant and possibly ignored? Only as you begin to understand the influence those table times have had on you can you make positive changes that will impact future generations.

CHAPTER 3

The Family Table

The Bible is filled with accounts connecting the importance and the influence of shared meals. In fact, the first recorded story of sin centered around disobedience to a dietary command. God told Adam and Eve that they could eat from any tree in the garden of Eden, except from the Tree of Knowledge of Good and Evil. All other fruits or vegetables were freely at the first couple's fingertips; they could eat whatever they chose. But Adam and Eve ingested the forbidden fruit, and families have suffered the consequences of those actions ever since.[17] Years later, a delicious meal was at the center of Rebekah and her son Jacob's deception of Isaac. The aging father, in a far-reaching, fascinating incident, was duped by Jacob and Rebekah, when Jacob pawned himself off as his slightly older twin brother,

Esau, to obtain by subterfuge Isaac's blessing of the firstborn. That devious meal changed the course of human history.

Certainly, meaningful meals also show up positively in Scripture. The entire Jewish sacrificial system revolved around food and feasting, with God's people celebrating together—sometimes for days at a time—and sharing their cherished history and values with their children. The Shema, one of the most revered truths in the Old Testament—"Hear O Israel, the LORD is our God, the LORD is one!"—is followed immediately by instructions to teach the words of God to our children:

> Hear, O Israel! The LORD is our God, the LORD is one! You shall love the LORD your God with all your heart and with all your soul and with all your might. These words, which I am commanding you today, shall be on your heart. You shall teach them diligently to your sons and shall talk of them when you sit in your house and when you walk by the way and when you lie down and when you rise up. You shall bind them as a sign on your hand and they shall be as frontals on your forehead. You shall write them on the doorposts of your house and on your gates.[18]

God intends parents to be the primary faith-trainers of our children, and one of the best places to implement this is "when you sit in your house": when your family is gathered around the table for a meal.

It's Not about When; It's about *Why*

Interestingly, there is nothing special about the time of day that you gather your family members around the table, only that you do. In the United States today, we tend to think of the dinner hour happening between 5:00 p.m. and 8:00 p.m. But historically, that hasn't always been the case.

In Colonial days, farming families got up at dawn or earlier, so they had their largest meal around 10:00 a.m. Even today, in some countries, the main meal of the day is eaten at midday, while in Latin American countries, the last meal is often eaten as late as 10:00 p.m.![19]

Author Cody C. Delistraty contends that the exact time when you eat with your family is more of a social custom than a hard-and-fast rule. "With all the studies and psychological findings about families who eat together in the evenings, we tend to think our best parenting, our essential bonding, happens around the dinner table at 6:00 p.m."[20] On the contrary, Delistraty points out that there is no such magical hour. In her book *Three Squares: The Invention of the American Meal*, Abigail Carroll seems to agree: "The family dinner as we think of it is relatively new—only about 150 years old. The ritual of coming together around a table in the evening is not a natural phenomenon; it is a social construction."[21]

Regardless of the time of day they gathered, families adopted the idea of meals being more meaningful than merely eating food to survive, although it took a while for parents to encourage their children to communicate more openly around the table. Food historian Mackensie Griffin likewise noted that the dining room transitioned from a more formal expression of togetherness, where children were expected to remain stoic and reserved, to a time for all members to express themselves and connect.[22]

Abigail Carroll discovered that in many generations, children at the table were not encouraged to speak their opinions or frustrations as is so highly prized today. "A 1744 etiquette manual titled *A Little Pretty Pocket Book* even warned children—lest they be tempted—not to speak unless spoken to."[23] It was not until the mid-nineteenth century that the dinner table was seen as an extension of a child's education and thus matters of manners and morality began to be taught at the table.[24]

While this appears as some revolutionary discovery, we know from Scripture that this wasn't the first time families discovered the power of mealtime connections. In Psalm 128, one of the blessings of God's people is seeing their children, like olive shoots, gathered around the table: "Your wife shall be like a fruitful vine within your house, your children like olive plants around your table" (v. 3 NASB).

Such imagery evokes the idea of healthy conversation and joy as opposed to rigid silence. Even the initial instructions for the Passover in Exodus 12 instruct the parents with what to say when their children ask why they are carrying out such traditions. This makes it clear that the children are fully engaged in both the ritual and conversation of mealtimes. The table is intended to be a blessing for all generations.

Where do you start with your family? Changing your world can start right there at your table, when you commit to having five meaningful mealtimes together each week. Recognize that your family mealtimes will define your family's future and make a firm, conscious decision that you want mealtimes to have a positive effect. Make up your mind: *I want to do this. I have to do this for the life of my family! I want our family to have five meaningful mealtimes together each week, and I'm willing to do whatever it takes to make that happen.*

What Makes Family Mealtimes Meaningful?

Shortly before the birth of Lily, our third daughter, Lana and I went on a Mediterranean cruise followed by a few extra days in Italy. We quickly noticed a contrast between the meals we ate in Italy and those we were accustomed to eating in many restaurants in the United States. In Italy, the meal is an *event*. The family and guests usually dress well for the meal, not necessarily in evening wear, but certainly not jeans and T-shirts. The group may not sit down to dinner until eight o'clock in the evening, and the meal may take at least two to three hours. The family lingers long after the food is consumed, conversing, telling stories, laughing, and simply enjoying being together.

In almost every restaurant where Lana and I ate, the people who were sitting at tables when we were being seated were still there as we were exiting the restaurant. No doubt they were wondering about us, "Why are you in such a hurry?"

I thought, *Maybe we need to learn something about how we do meals.*

For many Americans, eating together as a family is not regarded as special. It is simply something we do as a last resort, when we are not eating with friends or business associates. When we do eat with family members, it is often a rushed, mindless, meaningless routine that we do so we can prepare to do something else that we regard as more important.

"What's for dinner tonight?" "I'm hungry, let's eat." "I'm in a hurry. I have to go."

Sound familiar?

Many families are so involved with school or church activities, with Mom or Dad or the kids scurrying off in all directions, they are accustomed to hurrying through their mealtimes. No wonder we have so many commercials on television about heart disease and other ailments!

In contrast, long meals in homes and restaurants in Italy are the norm. Usually, the entire family is involved. The mealtimes are not hurried, rushed, or distracted. Unlike many American homes these days where we have meals with the television blaring in the background, or sometimes in the foreground, with people texting, checking email on their phones, or scrolling down through social media accounts or the news of the day, the mealtimes in Italy are considered sacrosanct—distractions are not appreciated. The family mealtime is a social event.

That is the first of three qualities that make a mealtime meaningful.

Meaningful Mealtimes Are Scheduled

Most of us really don't want to eat alone. We prefer to eat together with other people—especially people we enjoy. But like any event, mealtimes need to be on the calendar or they won't happen regularly. Everyone in the family should know when, where, and at what time you are going to eat. Make it a habit that everyone shows up on time and remains at the table until the time of discussion is completed. If you don't remain committed to eating together with your family or won't stick to it, it won't last.

If you don't get intentional about having five meaningful meals together each week, they won't happen.

But it's not as though this is something extraordinary. That's one of the reasons why mealtimes can be such powerful faith-and-family builders. All of your family members are already eating meals *somewhere*. So make a plan to eat them together!

Incidentally, there's a reason why my challenge is to eat five meaningful mealtimes with people you love—rather than specifically with your direct family members. Many people don't have direct access to family members, either because of their season of life or because others in their family aren't interested in engaging in this process. If you're single, or others in your family aren't committed to this practice, don't give up and eat alone! Be *extra* intentional about finding some other people in your life who would also benefit from regular times of eating together, and make that commitment. You might need to initiate the invitation with others who are in similar seasons of life and would benefit from such gatherings. In fact, you might seek out a family in your church, neighborhood, or community who you could welcome into your home.

Successful mealtimes come from commitment, not from creativity. Certainly, you can be as innovative and creative in planning your mealtimes as you want to be (or have time to be), but understand, it is not about doing something exotic or strange. It is simply about getting your family all together around the table without distractions.

If you want mealtimes with your family to be a priority, the meals together must be on your family members' calendars or they probably won't happen. In other words, *you* have to show up, and unless there is some vitally important reason, *all* of the family members should be expected to attend family mealtimes. But don't make it a rigid rule. Make it fun. Don't fret about having a perfect meal. Gathering the family together around the table should be a celebration time, something that you look forward to, and as your kids grow up, you will be creating good memories with your family.

Hopefully, the family walks away saying or thinking, "That wasn't merely physically nutritious; that was life-giving."

Let me caution you, though: If you don't stick to the idea that these meals are important, they won't be. If you don't get intentional about having these times together, it is highly unlikely that they will happen regularly.

But remember: It is not as though you are attempting to do something that is extraordinary. That's one of the reasons why mealtimes can be such powerful faith builders. You are already doing it—everyone has to eat—so simply plan to eat together as a family.

Meaningful Mealtimes Are Special

A second matter of importance must be that *meaningful mealtimes are special*. Not that you need to have a fancy feast or a Thanksgiving-style dinner at every meal. That's not what makes the mealtime special. It is special because of the people around the table and the spirit of the meal. Seek ways to make your family mealtime something that everyone looks forward to experiencing. Simply put, it ought to be fun and enjoyable for all, including the cook!

But don't mistake *special* with *difficult*. A special mealtime is not the same thing as an elaborate meal together. In fact, it can be quite simple and still be special. We paralyze ourselves with ridiculous, unnecessary standards. It is not so much about the food, the decor, or the *wow* factor that makes this time special. It is the people at the table, gathering together five times a week to simply enjoy eating and sharing together as a family.

You don't need to "put on airs" or pretend that your home is a page out of a homemaker's magazine. Just be yourself and do what feels natural for you and your family. If that is a gourmet dinner, fine! But if it is mac and cheese or hamburgers and hotdogs, that's okay too. What matters is that you are eating together as a family.

Much of what we learn about home life in various times throughout history is revealed by examining the art from those times. Judith Flanders's book *The Making of Home* discussed the history of seventeenth-century Dutch painters and the content of their works.[25] Many of the art pieces depict Mom and Dad and kids dressed immaculately, sitting around luxurious, perfectly set tables placed perfectly on beautiful Turkish rugs below extravagant chandeliers, all surrounded by exquisite marble floors. Oh, yeah, there is also the perfect, distinguished-looking family dog in many of the paintings.

But historians discovered a problem: the people portrayed in those paintings didn't really own all those fancy possessions! When the historians inventoried homes after the patriarchs had passed away, and all their possessions were catalogued, they discovered that the family home had dirt floors and was lucky to have two chairs and a table. They didn't have all the accouterments shown in the paintings. They just rented them for the picture. Those were "sets" used while the family posed for the painting, not real life. But they painted their families with many possessions as though they actually lived that way.

Today we have Instagram, Pinterest, and all sorts of other artificial social media featuring airbrushed, photoshopped images of family life depicting the "perfect" family. But there is no such thing as a perfect family, and most people realize those social media images are distortions, not reality.

Worse yet, they are so unnecessary! Stop trying to live up to a fictitious standard. Just enjoy dinner with your family. It doesn't have to be a four-course, home-cooked, gourmet meal.

And it doesn't even have to be at home. You can have a meaningful meal at an inexpensive fast-food restaurant. You can count a meal out at a restaurant as one of your five meaningful mealtimes—if, indeed, it is that. As long as your family is together without distractions, it can be a meaningful and valuable time. Just enjoy dinner together. And you need not restrict your family times to dinner. You may find that the best time to get your family members all in the same room is in the morning. Great! Do that. Any meal can be special time with your family.

Keeping mealtimes special might call for a few "family rules" for the meal. For instance, your mealtimes should be technology-free. That means no televisions, telephones, laptops, games, or other electronic gizmos. No screens allowed. Music, if included at all, should be soothing and in the background—far in the background so as not to impede conversations.

Your meaningful mealtime should not include side conversations with friends or even other family members who may be in the room but not at the table. No, this is a time for looking each other in the eye and communicating with one another around the table.

As an indication of respect for all, everyone should show up at the table on time. Certainly, schedule conflicts happen, but as a rule, plan to be at your family mealtime at the designated time, and stick to that plan.

Make mealtimes the social event of the day that you and your family members look forward to with joy.

Meaningful Mealtimes Are Spiritual

Your family mealtimes should involve more than merely eating food together. This is an excellent time to attach something of eternal, spiritual value to one of the most common, human things we do, and one of the best ways to do that is to engage in casual conversations about God and faith as you eat. This is not a time to debate theology or to argue over differences of opinion. On the other hand, you need not always talk about trivial, trite, transient tripe either! Don't be bashful about discussing great books and stories, movies, or music. And you can do more around the table than the "strip-mine" approach, skimming off the top layers. Slow down, take time to contemplate conversations about life, death, our purpose, where we came from, why we are here, where we are going—all of those and more are open for discussion.

What does that look like?

It might look different for your family than it does for ours, but most importantly, these special, spiritual events should be natural to you and your family.

Some of my favorite childhood memories are times spent with my parents around the dinner table. I felt so "grown up" when Mom and Dad included me in the conversation. Now, as a parent, some of my favorite memories of raising our daughters have been unhurried moments and conversations around our dinner table. Although our daughters Ryley and Reagan are now adults, as they were growing up, those times around the table were always some of the best opportunities to talk about what was going on in their lives and also to share serious—and sometimes not-so-serious—discussions about our faith.

It might surprise you that Lana and I did not institute regular family devotion times when our daughters were young. Devotions didn't work for us. I was a preacher and Lana was a schoolteacher, so when we tried to have devotional times around the table, they naturally turned into lesson plans. Whether they meant to or not, the kids usually tuned out. "Dad, can you put away the sermon?"

Perhaps, because I am a pastor, those few occasions when we attempted to pawn off family devotions as a natural part of our day always seemed to come off a bit stilted or contrived. Usually, at my most "spiritual" moment, Lana or one of the girls would crack a joke, and everything would go downhill from there. All sense of profound spiritual insights dissolved in seconds, and I'd grow frustrated that I couldn't be a more profound spiritual leader for my family.

It wasn't that my family members weren't interested in discussing more about God. They simply preferred real conversations over hype and hoopla.

Lana is a wonderful cook, but ironically, the meals our girls ask for when they return home are some of the simplest. One of Reagan's favorites is a Doritos casserole that Lana got from Pinterest. There's not much to it relative to some of the great food she's prepared, but that's what they remember most fondly. The same seems to be true as it relates to the formality of our talks around the table. I learned that the best devotions for us were found in everyday conversations that happened naturally as we enjoyed a meal together. Lana was my strongest advocate in this, keeping it real as she tenaciously and consistently gathered us together as a family at mealtimes, making it obvious to all of us that mealtimes were priorities in our family schedules.

We often asked our daughters to share one high point from their day and one low point from their day. They enjoyed telling us things that mattered to them, and our conversations felt more organic and natural.

We discussed everything from the serious to the seriously mundane. Sometimes we'd joke about something or discuss an important family matter. We'd join together in discussing a report that one of the girls was scheduled to give at school, some preparation for an athletic event, or something that was happening at church. Lana and I tried to balance the conversations, making sure our daughters' interests were high on our lists, not merely our always-busy church activities schedule.

Although meaningful mealtimes should be spiritual, there's no need to squeeze "God talk" into every conversation; just be natural about it. But be aware and intentional about it too. Look for those ordinary opportunities to evoke conversations about God, Jesus, Christianity, and how faith plays out in relationships in school or at work, and you might be amazed at what sticks.

Lana's Doritos™ Casserole

Ingredients:

2 cups cooked chicken, shredded or cubed

1 cup cheddar cheese, shredded

1 can cream of chicken soup

1/2 cup milk

1/2 cup sour cream

1 can RO-TEL tomatoes, drained

1/2 packet taco seasoning (or more to your taste)

11-ounce bag of regular Nacho Cheese Doritos

Instructions:

1. Preheat the oven to 350 degrees.
2. Grease an 8 x 8 baking dish.
3. Combine all the ingredients except the Doritos in a mixing bowl.
4. Put a layer of 2 cups of crumbled Doritos in the baking dish, followed by a layer of the chicken mixture. Repeat the layers, ending with chicken on top.
5. Top with additional shredded cheese.
6. Bake for 30–35 minutes.
7. Spoon the casserole onto plates and top with additional crumbled Doritos.

(Adapted from Jam Hands[26])

When our kids were in high school, we would sometimes watch TV shows together as a family that weren't necessarily spiritual but brought up real-life challenges that we could talk about in a way that seemed less confrontational or "lecture-based." As we passed around the entrees, a simple question would often get the words flowing around the dinner table: "Last night on the show, Julie chose to lie to her parents about where she'd been the night before. What were the advantages of that decision? What could go wrong?" It's amazing how much easier it is to talk about tough topics when they're in the context of a fictional drama. In fact, just bringing up difficult issues in the form of a question sets the table for success.

Still today, with our adult daughters, we may bring up a controversial topic, perhaps even one that I know our kids have different opinions about than those Lana and I share. Rather than immediately challenging their positions from my lofty, fatherly, know-it-all perch, I may say, "Help me understand what that means to you."

Mealtimes may be a natural opportunity for you to interact with your family members about things that really matter. I much prefer to hear what our kids have to say on a subject, and it is a double-win. They enjoy being heard, and I don't have to be the answer man. Even if the words come sparingly between bites, I'm convinced that the very best opportunity you have to connect with a teen is around a meal. Here's why: when the focus is off the conversation itself, the pressure is off as well. This doesn't have to be complicated. Here are some ways that have worked for many families:

- Use a simple question to help jump-start a longer conversation. Simply prime the pump of curiosity around the table: "If you could instantly master one sport or activity, what would it be?" (For me, I'd love to know how to play the cello! But that's another story . . .)

- Beyond a simple teaser like this, I'd recommend allowing *them* to lead out with the topics of conversation: you're hearing what is on their minds and letting the conversation flow in a natural way.
- If there's a prevalent topic in the news, you can bring it up and simply ask, "What do you think about what happened?"

But if working off a blank conversational canvas seems awkward to you, you can find some conversation starters at the back of this book. If these are helpful, we've posted hundreds more free online "Faith Talks" and other materials. You can find them at Empowered-Homes.org, a site we've assembled to strengthen families in every season of life. These "Faith Talks" aren't complicated, but they offer ideas that might lend some spiritual energy to the conversations around your table.

Having five meaningful meals with the people you love each week is such a priority to us, we encourage first-time visitors to our church to develop the habit. "We understand that Kingsland isn't for everybody," we acknowledge. "So if you are not comfortable here, we have a list of several other congregations nearby that we are happy to recommend to you, good Bible-based fellowships. But if you never come back to Kingsland, or you don't do anything else, please do this one thing: have five meaningful mealtimes with your family each week."

After their visit, we also send our guests a free pizza cutter and a coupon voucher for a free pizza at a cooperating business nearby. And we remind them again, "Please do one thing: have five meaningful meals with your family each week."

It is a simple but profound truth: healthy families eat together.

Taking on the Challenge

With two of our daughters on their own and living away from home, mealtimes at the Rush house have adapted to this season of life. Our youngest daughter is now moving into young adulthood, but her disabilities make our dinner table a little more unusual. In her early years, when Lily first received her autism diagnosis, she was lost in her own world with little connection to us or anyone else. We prayed and prayed for her to recover. While the answer didn't come exactly as we had hoped, and she still deals with numerous challenges, connection is not one of them. Lily has one of the sweetest smiles on earth, and I don't know anyone who can speak so clearly through her eye contact without saying a word.

I'm a little embarrassed to say that our despondency through some tough years reduced our own mealtimes to far less than they should have been. We used the hectic schedule involving therapy, doctor appointments, and ministry to justify the lack of time around the table. But the truth is, there were many days that sitting across the table from a daughter who was disengaged was painful, and we avoided the reminder of how different our lives had become from anything we expected.

A few years ago, however, during one of the evenings when we gathered uninterrupted around the table, Lily looked intently at her mom and me and folded her hands.

Lana said, "Lily, would you like to pray?"

Lily nodded intently. Lily has been reminding us ever since that there is something holy about our gatherings, unique as they may be in this season. Lily cannot speak, but she is totally engaged in the conversation. And I have to tell you: she has turned into the "prayer police." It doesn't matter who gathers around our table or where they stand in their faith journey, Lily will stare at each person until every head is bowed and all hands folded. Do you want seconds? Well, that will involve a brand new prayer.

I'm aware that there are plenty of families like ours in which the dinner experience is far from any classic painting. That doesn't mean you can't enjoy meaningful mealtimes. We use more repetition than we would with a typical child. If Lily has completed some artwork at church to help her remember a Bible story, we'll display it at the dinner table all week long. Sometimes we even hang it from the chandelier! But God can still bless the time. When there is someone in the family with a hearing impairment, visual cues become more important to help everyone focus. For Lily, that's a folding of the hands for prayer or a picture of our topic. These additions to the mealtime routine aren't just for special needs individuals, however. They can help all of us remember the significance of the meal.

We have some friends who light a candle at the table to remind their two young daughters that Jesus is the light of the world, and He is present at the meal.

No matter the obstacles you face, mealtimes can be a blessing for all involved if you just use a little creativity. We didn't give up at the Rush house. Lily wouldn't allow it.

CHAPTER 4

The Transforming Power of the Table

In his best-selling book, *Atomic Habits*, James Clear points out that most people assume the best way to change their habits is by setting goals. Instead, he asserts the most powerful way to form enduring habits is to focus not on your habits but on your *identity*—the way you see yourself and the essence of who you are. For example, if someone wants to begin working out and getting in shape, he may set goals to exercise four days a week. But Clear asserts a far more powerful first step would involve seeing oneself as a healthy person who likes to stay fit.[27] There's a huge difference between saying, "I'm a lazy guy, and I need to get in shape!" versus, "I'm a jogger, and it's not like me to miss out on my weekly routines!" These differences are subtle, and maybe even sound a bit like pop psychology, but truly special and transformational things happen when we see ourselves in a different light. More importantly, when we begin to see ourselves as God sees us, something wonderful happens. I am absolutely convinced that "ground zero" for shaping our identities can happen around the table.

One of the great blessings of my life has been the friendship I enjoyed with Dr. Ralph Smith, a brilliant man who served as the pastor of Hyde Park Baptist Church in Austin, Texas, for thirty-six years. I did not get to know Ralph until he had been retired for nearly a decade, but our paths crossed soon after Lana and I moved to Austin in 2002. We began meeting weekly to talk about life, ministry, family, and what it really meant to make our lives count for eternity. Moving to a new city meant I had left behind many of the wonderful mentors in my life and ministry. Ralph and I became fast friends, and he soon became that older mentor that every young pastor wants and needs. I'd like to think I, too, met a need in Ralph's life—to pour all of those life lessons into a younger man in the faith. Whether that was true or not, I was blessed!

Dr. Ralph passed away a few years ago, and I drove back to Austin to celebrate this extraordinary life that had touched mine and so many others. As I heard individuals speak so highly of his impact, I thought about this gift of friendship I had been given. It dawned on me in those moments that in all our precious times together, the vast majority were not "meetings" at all, but mealtimes. We'd meet for Mexican food at a run-down restaurant with average food that Ralph somehow thought was wonderful. I'd endure mediocre queso for an audience with my friend any day. Every now and then we'd branch out for a burger at another place or a steak on special occasions. But the food was never the point. The food was a gateway to the life lessons Ralph had experienced and was more than willing to pass along. Looking back, these tables were more than dinner tables. They were tables of transformation. And they changed my life.

There were many lunches where nothing magical happened; we were just two friends catching up and talking about the news of the day. But the deep connection that grew between us allowed us the freedom to go deeper. Ralph would share about his perspective as a retired pastor and, later, a widower. He would at times bring along a copy of a favorite sermon he had preached decades ago but still held power and wisdom. And some days, I'd pour my heart out about something that seemed like the end of the world. On those occasions, Ralph would give me a long, gracious look and say, "Ryan, listen. Are you listening? You're going to get through this. And you'll be better because of it." He was always right. My life and ministry would not have been the same without my friend Ralph, and I'm not sure our friendship would have been the same without that average Mexican food.

I think every mealtime has the potential to be more than a mealtime in this same way. There's something powerful about the learning that takes place in the midst of dining conversation, when the walls are down and the stories are passed along. It's no wonder that all these mealtime studies demonstrate the many benefits of such habits that have nothing to do with food. Are you ready to infuse your mealtimes with a higher purpose and goal?

Making your table transformational is not as complicated as it sounds. In fact, if you try to convert your mealtimes into classrooms, you'll find it might even be counterproductive. The power of mealtime training is that it *does not* feel like work! To be sure, if you're a parent, there are moments in which you need to equip your kids intentionally with foundational truth. You can't afford to merely hope they catch these essential elements: the faithfulness of God, the power of integrity, the value of hard work. As you utilize teaching moments, significant life milestones, and partnerships with a local church to impart your values, however, it is the casual nature of mealtimes that will help to write those values on their hearts.

The strong foundation of a healthy home makes all of our lives easier. The American Enterprise Institute looked at intact family units and published a study demonstrating that the highest prevalence of family structures that remain together have the lowest prevalence of crime, poverty, and health crises.[28] It's no wonder that God designed our families as the primary building block of society. The better the home life, the better the society. The philosopher Plato said, "The saga of a nation is the saga of its families," and that is true. We must get our homes right if we want our nation to be safer, more secure, more productive, and more civil.

Not that we are perfect, by any means. We are all broken people, so obviously we all live in broken homes. But if we truly want life to improve, we don't start with the government, Hollywood, or some other group; we can discover God's forgiveness and change the world, beginning right around our family dining table.

What do you want to accomplish during your five meaningful mealtimes each week? What can you do to make your mealtimes more purposeful? How can you get started? Transformation happens with intentionality and training.

Training Matters

The apostle Paul wrote to the young pastor Timothy, "Have nothing to do with pointless and silly myths. Rather, train yourself in godliness."[29] Every professional athlete is familiar with training camp, preparing for the new season and creating habits that will help maintain

fitness all through the year. And one of the most important features of a good athlete's training regimen is the
training *table* that is instrumental in bringing about that
transformation.

Paul encourages Timothy (and us) to engage in *spiritual* training. You don't have to go to a special location
for this training. Spiritual training can occur right in your
home around your dining table. If you have children, you
know the importance of teaching them not merely about
a good diet, healthy physical habits, and productive career
skills to survive in this world but also spiritual values that
will provide a foundation and a standard for living. You
can do that subtly over time as you consistently have five
meaningful mealtimes each week.

The apostle Paul gives a pattern to the Ephesian
church, where Timothy was a pastor, for imparting values, and this same pattern is evident throughout the
Bible. He names three steps that will help us develop our
spiritual training, growth, and maturity.

Step 1: Focus on the Person of Jesus Christ

The first step, Paul says, it to *focus on the person of Jesus
Christ*. In Ephesians 4, the apostle describes some people
whose minds have been darkened, who are living igno-
rant, hopeless lives and don't know God, so they have
engaged in negative actions and attitudes. Immediately

after that, Paul says, "But that is not how you came to know Christ."[30]

Interesting, isn't it, that Paul did not say that's not what you learned *from* Christ or even information *about* Jesus? He says that's not how you learned Christ Himself. Paul is saying that the beginning of spiritual training disciplines is not merely intellectual knowledge about Jesus. It is relational. Start with the person of Jesus Christ. The fancy word for this is *theology*, the study of God. It is not merely knowing the rules or acquiring more facts; it is the study of the nature and attributes of God. Paul says to study Him. The apostle encourages us to lay aside those old, selfish ways of living and "to put on the new self, the one created according to God's likeness in righteousness and purity of the truth."[31] That new self doesn't come by working harder to be a good person, following all the rules, or any self-effort. It comes as a result of being made into God's image.

The apostle continues in Ephesians 5:1 by saying, "Therefore be imitators of God, as beloved children" (ESV). Imitate God!

As you learn to imitate God, you have the privilege of reflecting the image of God—His nature. For instance, God is faithful, so I can be faithful; God is gracious, so I can show grace. God is righteous, so I can demonstrate doing right. If you want to change your life or help change your family members' lives, don't start by trying to figure out all the rules; start by reflecting God. Look to the person of Jesus Christ and ask, "Who is Jesus, and how did He live? How can I emulate Him? I want to imitate God."

It is as though you are a mirror, looking to Jesus and reflecting Him to others. What does the mirror reflect? It reflects whatever is facing it. Whatever you focus on—good or bad, positively or negatively—eventually you will imitate. God wired you that way so you could reflect Him.

If you look to God, you will attempt to mimic His character. If you focus on someone or something other than God, sooner or later, you will become like that person or thing.

How does this work around your table? Maybe you and your family are trying to have a meaningful mealtime, when one of the kids brings up the subject that somebody lied. Maybe it was a music artist who got caught lying to his or her marriage partner, or perhaps it was a political candidate who said one thing and did something else. Or maybe it was a student at school who told a "white lie." Regardless, it was a lie.

What can you do with that when it is mentioned at your table? Rather than piling on with the tabloids or the pundits, right there, you can choose to focus on God. You do that by drawing the conversation back to who God is.

"Let's go back and look at who Jesus is," you can suggest. "Jesus is righteous, He is holy, He is faithful, and that means He will do what He says He will do. Jesus is always truthful; He doesn't lie." In this manner, you can begin to redirect the conversation by looking to God and who He is rather than at the person who committed the lie.

This is one of the reasons why having meaningful mealtimes is so important. Whether you're a mom or a dad, a grandparent, or a friend trying to encourage someone, your family members, friends, or others gathered around your table are looking at you, hoping that you will reflect who God is and what Jesus would do. So you have an opportunity to show them who God is and what His character is like in your natural environment, on a regular basis, without any hype, hoopla, or confusing religious jargon. Just reflect Jesus.

Step 2: Look for the Promise of God

The second step to spiritual training is to *look for the promise of God.* The apostle Peter offers us some good news about God's provision: "His divine power has given us everything required for life and godliness through the knowledge of him who called us by his own glory and goodness."[32] That sounds a lot like what Paul said in Ephesians 4, doesn't it? We've been given access to the power of God for our lives in a very specific way: through the "knowledge of him who called us"—Jesus Christ. As we know more of Jesus, we gain more power for living.

But that leaves us with an important question: Even as we get to know Jesus better, *how* does that transfer into power for our lives? Well, Peter is glad you asked! He answers that question in the next verse:

"By these he has given us very great and precious promises, so that through them you may share in the divine nature, escaping the corruption that is in the world because of evil desire."[33]

Our love grows deeper as we know more of Jesus. Our lives grow stronger as we know more of the promises He has made. Based on an understanding of who God is, you are invited to seek the truth and the promises that flow out of His character.

Because of who He is, we can ask, "What has He promised us?" and take our direction from there. For instance, because God is faithful, He has promised never to leave you or forsake you. So when you are going through difficult times, you can look to those promises that He will be faithful to you.

I've already shared that our youngest daughter, Lily, is disabled. When she turned four years old, it began to dawn on us that we weren't just dealing with a few passing medical problems; there were likely going to be chronic needs for the rest of her life. On one day when we received another dose of particularly devastating news, Lana and I were sitting on the floor of Lily's bedroom watching her play with a toy while we cried together—trying to get our minds around how we could move forward. I remember hearing a whisper from God that said, "What have I promised you?" I relayed this to Lana and suggested that we think about it and actually say out loud the promises God had made us as they came to mind. (To clarify, there was no trace of a "suck it up" tone in this invitation. We were both grieving, and we desperately needed an anchor in that moment.)

We moved the discussion from the floor of Lily's bedroom to the kitchen, made some sandwiches for lunch, and sat down with a new determination to remember the truth about God and the situation we were in. I suppose we could have had the same discussion anywhere, but the kitchen table brought us face-to-face with each other in a place we had preconditioned for spiritual discussion. And to be honest, the sandwiches took a little of the edge off. For the next forty-five minutes God began to lift our hearts as we spoke the promises we knew to be true—out loud to each other.

"I know that God will never leave us or forsake us."

"I know that He who began a good work in Lily will be faithful to complete it until the day of Christ Jesus."

"I know that all these things work together for the good of those who love God, who are called according to His purpose."

That moment turned out to be a turning point in our family life—not because I asked some profound question, but because we gathered at the table and began to home in on what we knew to be true rather than the roller coaster of emotions we were feeling.

Step 3: Develop the Practice of Obedience

The third step in your spiritual training is to *develop the practice of obedience.*

After he reminds us that we are called to learn Christ and then be taught in Him, the apostle Paul tells us to "take off your former way of life, the old self that is corrupted by deceitful desires, to be renewed in the spirit of your minds, and to put on the new self, the one created according to God's likeness in righteousness and purity of the truth."[34]

This is where mealtimes can become a transformational tool for growth in every home: when we connect the dots between the character and nature of Jesus, the promises of Jesus, and the practical steps we can take to walk in those promises.

When our kids were in late elementary school, Lana and I initiated "sticky situation" conversations around our mealtime table. Sometimes, we placed a jar full of discussion questions in the center of the dinner table and let the kids pull out a question at each mealtime to talk about. At other times, we'd raise issues that we were pretty certain our daughters had not yet encountered—but we knew they would eventually. We'd set up a situation like this: "You are at a party with your teenage friends and someone brings in a six-pack of beer, or pulls out some joints and begins smoking marijuana, or even injects a drug. What are you going to do if that happens?"

"Oh, Dad! Oh, Mom!" the girls would say. "That's not going to happen with our friends."

"Okay, I hope not. But what are you going to do if it does?"

"I'm not going to do that!"

"But what if your friends make fun of you for not joining them? Then what?"

Lana and I purposely set up hypothetical scenarios where our kids might be in uncomfortable situations, and then we let them talk about potential solutions.

Interestingly, years later, on more than a few occasions as our daughters grew into their late teens, one of them would come home and say, "Dad! Mom! It happened. It happened just like you said!"

Take advantage of any opportunity to add a faith element to your kids' day. As our girls were growing up, one of my responsibilities was dropping them off at school each morning. When our daughters reached for the door handle to get out of the car, I took that moment to remind them who they were.

"Ryley, Reagan, remember what I asked you to do today. What is it?"

"Change the world."

"Yes, that's it."

It was less than twenty seconds each day, but Ryley and Reagan grew up with the attitude that God had a significant purpose for them to fulfill. They were born to help change the world for the better.

They didn't acquire that concept automatically. Quite the contrary, Lana and I consciously poured into them a concern and compassion for the world through conversations at every meal around the table.

Recently, Reagan and I were reminiscing about some of the "sticky situations" that Lana or I posed for our daughters. "Dad, what did you think we were going to say while at dinner with you?" Reagan asked with a laugh.

No doubt, some of our sticky situations seemed naive or contrived to the kids. And they were! But they were good conversation starters and our daughters loved it when we simply talked about life, giving them our undivided attention as they expressed their opinions.

Our goal was to get our girls to follow Paul's practical instructions here: to do things out of who God is and the truth they knew through Jesus. That would guide them in how to live in everyday, practical ways as they obeyed God's instructions. These three steps are the pattern for training and discipleship, and they can be discovered in various places throughout the Bible.

Keep the Order Straight

The pattern is not complicated, but the sequence in which you approach your training table is important. It is not arbitrary, random, or willy-nilly. No, the pattern, if you expect it to work in every area of your life, must be done in sequence.

This pattern shows up frequently in the Bible. Consider the important truth we looked at in Deuteronomy 6, a foundational parenting passage: "Hear, O Israel: the Lord our God, the Lord is one" (v. 4 NASB). Notice, it doesn't start by saying, "Do these things with your kids." It begins by drawing our attention to the person of God—that is, who is He? From there, God says that these commands He gives are to be on your heart and mind. That means when we wonder what is really true in this life, we know where to turn—to God's Word, the truth He has given to us. Then from there, you move to the last step, "You shall teach them diligently to your children" (v. 7 ESV).

These same steps are essential when it comes to living the Christian life. God wants us to start with the person of Jesus, then build on the promises He has given us, and then develop the practice of obedience, living like Jesus in our homes and in society.

This is not a list that you can check off and then you are done. No, this is a lifetime worth of discovery as you explore what it means to know Jesus, to trust His promises, and to do the things He tells you to do.

Did you ever study psychologist Abraham Maslow's hierarchy of needs? In creating a pyramid showing what motivates people, Maslow laid his foundational needs with such things as food and shelter, then moved up to other needs such as belonging, esteem, and self-actualization. But if you don't address the foundation, you can't build or move higher.

Our spiritual training is similar. If you focus on the three steps but choose a different order, you will short-circuit the power, and your growth in Christ will be stunted. No matter what you want to accomplish at the spiritual training table, if you get the order out of whack, it simply won't work. In fact, if you try to do the spiritual training steps in a different order, that approach will probably be debilitating for you and counterproductive for your family.

For instance, if you implement the practice of obedience without really understanding who God is or what sort of promises He has made to you, most likely you will slide into legalism—trying to keep all the rules so God will like you—or burnout, exhausted in trying to please the God you don't really know.

Similarly, if you emphasize God's promises without understanding His character, you can easily get distracted by pride or guilt. When the truth of God's promises are disconnected from the character of Jesus, they begin to feel a lot like rules. When we abide by rules, we can end up feeling pretty great about ourselves. When we fail to obey, we wind up feeling terrible. But when those rules are seen instead as loving commands given by a God who knows us deeply, we can set aside either pride or guilt and choose *gratitude* instead. Do you see? God's promises are *deeply* rooted in His character.

If you focus first on the person of Jesus, you will have a much better reason to believe His promises and to obey His instructions.

Some people get the steps out of order and then wonder why they aren't growing. So many real-life conversations as a pastor come to mind. I think of Bart, who proclaimed, "I want to grow in Christ, I want to go deeper with God, so I just need to know more. I am going to read my Bible more and study more so I can have a deeper relationship with God."

Wide-eyed Sherry, a relatively new believer in Jesus, put it this way: "Yes, I am going to start with the promises and maybe through them I can get access to God. So I'm going to check out all the promises of God so I can claim them for myself, and from that, I can obey what He tells me to do."

While both Bart and Sherry may have had the best of intentions, they were sabotaging their own spiritual training. Without some adjustment to their strategies, their efforts would have inevitably produced an unhealthy walk with the Lord.

Why? Because if we think the path to relationship with God lies through our knowledge, we usually plunge into "religion," which sounds like Christianity but it is not. Christianity is about the *relationship* you can have with Jesus Christ, not merely learning about and performing the requirements of a religion.

That sort of spiritual training will fall apart of its own weight, perhaps crushing you under a pile of legalistic rules, regulations, and "spiritual" requirements in the process. The result is not healthy spiritual training; it is pride, or guilt for not keeping your pledge, often leading to spiritual disillusionment and burnout.

Think back to that conversation around the table when the topic came up about somebody lying. If you have the training steps out of sequence, how are you likely to respond?

"In this family, we do not lie."

Now that sounds good, doesn't it?

Until someone asks, "*Why* don't we lie? Lots of people who lie seem to get ahead in the world. Why shouldn't we lie?"

"Well, because bad people lie. And we are not bad people."

That sounds reasonable, too, doesn't it?

Until the first time that somebody sins. And we discover that we are all broken, bad people apart from the forgiveness of God and our redemption purchased for us by the blood of Jesus Christ on the cross. So don't set your family up for failure by saying, "Just suck it up and do what is right. Just be good, for goodness' sake."

The problem with being good for goodness' sake is that your righteousness will last only as long as the guilt does. Then when you realize that you can't be good on your own, you slide into spiritual despair, and that is dangerous to your physical, emotional, and spiritual health.

Rather than risking that downward spiral, God has invited us to focus first on the person of Jesus Christ. "I want to run to Him," we say. "I want to know Him and have a relationship with Him. Out of that relationship, I want to look to His promises and learn to trust Him, that He loves me and has my best interests at heart, and out of His promises, I want to practice doing the things He instructs me to do—not out of fear of disobedience but out of the sheer joy in my relationship with Jesus."

This same pattern is seen even in God's giving of the Ten Commandments. In Exodus 20, before a single commandment was shared, God said, "I am the LORD your God" (v. 2). Notice, He begins with reminding us who He is. Surprisingly, perhaps, He doesn't simply say, "I am

God, so pay attention." No, He says, "I am *your* God," using the term of endearment and personal relationship, showing that He has a relationship with each of His people. "I am *your* God."

He then proceeds to remind His people of His promises. "I am the LORD your God, who brought you out of the land of Egypt, out of the house of slavery."[35] He had promised to deliver His people, and He did it when He brought them out of slavery and bondage and into freedom.

Then—and only then—does He go on to give His people commandments and instructions to obey. But the commandments don't bring about the relationship; His people are meant to obey the commandments *because* of their relationship with God.

We are mistaken if we look at the Ten Commandments and say, "Well, these are the rules that God has given us so we can get to Him, so we can have a relationship with Him."

No, He begins with "I am the Lord your God" and you have rules because of our relationship. That is a totally different way of living compared to trying to earn your way into God's presence by keeping all the rules.

So when issues arise and you have meaningful conversations with your family around your dining table, it is incredibly liberating if you go back to the person of Jesus, discover His promises, and out of that relationship, say,

"Let's look at what the Lord has done for us. Now, how can we practice walking in obedience to Him?"

You can apply these steps to any challenge, but keep in mind the goal of the steps. Remember what Paul said? He encouraged the Ephesians, "Therefore be imitators of God, as beloved children; and walk in love, just as Christ also loved you and gave Himself up for us, an offering and a sacrifice to God as a fragrant aroma."[36]

Did you get that picture? Imitate God as His beloved children. That's what kids do—they imitate their parents. Little girls love to dress up in mommy's clothes or parade around the house in her shoes. Little boys want to wear superhero costumes and go out like daddy to conquer the world. By imitating mom and dad, the children slowly grow into adulthood.

Paul is saying, "Do something similar with God. Imitate God, walk in His love. Start your training by asking, 'Who is God? Oh, I see, Jesus is God. Okay, I want to be like Jesus.'" In fact, this is another reason why the table is such a powerful tool in this process. You have a "base" where your family can look forward to gathering, a safe place where conversations can begin and then be set aside for a day or two without being forgotten. The table is a natural incubator for ideas about life and the perfect place for picturing a future of walking in God's promises. When you begin to see mealtimes as more than a chance to satisfy your stomach, you'll look forward to these moments with a renewed anticipation.

In fact, notice the goal of the three steps is not obedience; it is *passion*! Passionate love! Passionate joy! That's when the Christian life becomes fun. This passionate, loving, joyful way of living is totally antithetical to merely keeping the rules or doing the bare minimum to get by.

Training at Jesus's Table

These three training table steps created a conundrum for Thomas, one of Jesus's disciples, the night before Jesus went to the cross. On the occasion of the Last Supper, the disciples were coming to grips with their questions about Jesus. He had already told them at various times that He was going to die and then three days later arise from the dead, but the disciples couldn't comprehend that radical message. They were grappling with their dashed dreams that Jesus would become a king, overthrow the Roman oppressors, and deliver Israel. But now the disciples were faced with the ominous truth, that Jesus was going to become their sacrifice, their Lamb to pay the price for their sin.

Jesus said, "Don't let your heart be troubled. Believe in God; believe also in me. . . . I am going to prepare a place for you."[37]

Thomas, who later became known for his skepticism and doubt, voiced what the others were probably thinking as well. Thomas asked, "Lord, we don't know where you're going. . . . How can we know the way?"[38]

That term *Lord* may mean "sir," and it can also be used of royalty. Thomas was trying to wrap his mind around the question, *Who is this Jesus? If He is supposed to be a king—the King—I'm having a dilemma. Who is God?*

Thomas had seen Jesus do miraculous things. But was his King going to submit to crucifixion and death?

"We don't know where you are going," he said to Jesus. In other words, "I'm trying to get my mind around Your promise that You are preparing a place for us, but I don't understand."

"How can we know the way?" Thomas continued. Of course, what he was asking on a deeper level was, "What am I supposed to do? I don't understand Your lordship, I don't know where You are going, so I don't know what I am supposed to do. I don't know who God is now, and I don't know what's true, and I don't know why I am here. Jesus, can You help me with these things?"

Have you ever been there? Yep, me too. Most of us have.

Jesus answered all three of Thomas's questions with one reply. He stated clearly, "I am the way, the truth, and the life. No one comes to the Father except through me."[39]

Who is God? If you want to know God and His character, Jesus said, "I am the way."

Do you want to know the truth in life? Jesus said that He is the Way you can discover to what really matters, what is really true."

Do you want to know what to do with your life? Jesus said, "I *am* the life."

Perhaps you have been focusing on the wrong thing to make your mealtimes more special. After all, there are plenty of ideas available for families today: I've seen books about cooking together (which isn't a bad idea), videos about setting the table in fun ways as a family, and blogs about preparing kids' food in fun shapes and colors. All of these might be great suggestions, but they're probably not going to change lives. If you want to see something transformational take place around the table, look to Jesus and discover who God really is. Maybe you've gotten the training steps out of order, trying to work harder, learn more, and claim more of God's promises without truly knowing who He is. God is calling you from religion to a real relationship with Him. The choice is yours, and if you will trust Him, you can find life—a life of forgiveness, salvation, and freedom—and your kids can, too, as you model this transformation around your table.

CHAPTER 5

A Table Reclaimed

Imagine a woman earnestly working in her woodshop. She's arranging the broken pieces of an old wooden table—even those that were damaged, disfigured, or stained—and lovingly preparing to do the hard task of restoration. She sands the marred wood, repairs the broken pieces and mends them back together where possible, and carefully replaces the hardware. Finally, she covers the finished product with a fresh coat of lacquer, and what once seemed lost comes back to life. In fact, many would consider this "new" table more precious than the former one.

Our friends, Gene Larson and Joanne White, did this very restorative work in Wimberley, Texas, the town where Lana and I met. For many years, they would seek out used or broken furniture that others regarded as junk. Gene and Joanne would rework the marred pieces, sand them down, fix any flaws, and turn them into masterpieces.

Gene and Joanne have a rich legacy of restoring what other people may have seen as hopeless. Our family has several pieces of Gene and Joanne's reclaimed furniture in our home. People who visit our family often see their craftsmanship and remark, "What a beautiful piece of furniture!"

"It's better than that," I'll say. "It is a beautiful piece of furniture that was once on a trash heap, but someone saw it and recognized its potential. With the touch of the master's hand, it has been reclaimed—saved and renewed."

We're so quick to cast off people, but God pulls people off the trash heap and turns them into masterpieces. Others may see us as junk, but God sees what we can be, not merely what we have been or how we have missed the mark.

That is God's Father-heart. God sees our potential. He not only understands what has happened to you in the past and what you are working through in the present; God sees the person you will be in the future.

Your mealtimes have the potential to play an important role in bringing restoration to the areas of your life that may seem beyond repair. Day after day, you get to rewrite your legacy around tables, sharing your life story, your concerns, and your dreams with those near you. All of us likely have some wounds from the past that still elicit painful memories, and many of those memories are tied to the table in one of two ways. For some, the table was a reminder of who was *not* present and should have been. Perhaps the table was a place of tension and unspoken conflict. For other people, even in the darkest periods of their lives, the table was a safe haven. It was a place of encouragement and healing. Regardless, you need to know that God can help you reclaim the table experiences in your past. Better yet, there doesn't have to be pain associated with your family's table in the future. But before the table can be redeemed (which we will get to in a later chapter), it must first be reclaimed. When a family reclaims and "owns" the table, it creates all sorts of opportunities for good things to happen.

Most of us would like to see our family members thrive. One of the simplest ways for that to happen is by reclaiming the table—the breakfast, lunch, and dinner table.

Why do you need to "reclaim" mealtimes at your home? Because what used to be natural now must be intentional.

Until relatively recent history, mom and dad were almost always home for meals with the children and other family members. That was the primary time and location where families connected—at mealtimes. Families met around the dinner table—mom, dad, and kids. If the family wanted to eat, they gathered at the kitchen or dining room table.

Then came the 1700s and the Industrial Revolution, and for the first time in history, dad went into the factory to work and was often absent at mealtime.

Our children used to learn from mom and dad simply by watching them and listening to them. We often say, "Christianity must be caught, not merely taught." And in the early years of our nation that happened quite naturally for many families as they gathered for their mealtimes. But then during the 1800s, parents began sending their kids off somewhere else, and to someone else, to educate them. Rather than mom and dad educating their children, other people—with their own ideas, values, agendas, and personal baggage—became the primary educators of our children. Listen: I'm grateful for all the advances we have made in education over the centuries. However, we cannot deny the reality that because parents are often not the primary academic trainers in the lives of their children, part of the faith training that used to happen in the course of such instruction no longer involves mom and dad, and *what used to be natural now must be intentional*.

Exacerbating matters further, in the 1940s, massive numbers of men went off to war, as did many women who went to work to support the troops and their families. Both men and women emerged from the war with all sorts of PTSD and emotional separation issues. Harvard University conducted a longitudinal study of the lives of World War II veterans that has proven this to be more than conjecture, demonstrating that a large percentage of these individuals suffered from emotional trauma, oftentimes resulting in separation problems.[40] The God-designed attachment process that forged meaningful connections between a child and her parents was disrupted for many in the following generations.

How often have you heard, "Dad never told us he loved us. He showed us by working hard and providing for us, but he never said the words. Dad was never good at loving out loud." Many of the children of that generation—who are now parents and grandparents themselves—nod their heads in agreement. "That's just the way it was," they say. That may be understandable, but in truth, it often meant that dad had never dealt with his own mess; he had never experienced a breakthrough. He simply submerged all the hurt and pain in his life and passed on similar admonitions to the next generation. "Be tough. Suck it up, and be a man." Those were the adages with which most sons of the Greatest Generation grew up.

What is furthering the separation in our families now? It is a relational separation, thanks to our addiction to technology and social media. We now have online relationships with people hundreds of miles away but can't look eye to eye with someone across the table from us.

Add to that the dehumanizing effects of the sexual revolution in the 1960s and the millions who carry scars from loved ones who sought pleasure over commitment, and you can understand why emotional separation affects relationships so negatively. While some claim that sexual liberation has freed them to "love whoever they want," the truth is, our culture's attitudes toward sexuality have resulted in horrendous pain and abuse for many.

Adding to the confusion about what a family really is based on, consider what is depicted in modern movies or television shows—an image of the traditional family that is frequently and intentionally twisted by those in Hollywood and elsewhere, who have their own agendas and ideas about what a "modern family" ought to be. It is easy to understand why so many people today are confused about gender issues, roles in society, and how to treat each other with kindness and respect.

We have lost the family table, and we need to reclaim it.

Start with Your Table

The most important step toward reclaiming the table from past hurts and baggage is to begin with your *own* table, avoiding the temptation to invest that energy on blame and regret. Today, you have the opportunity to begin using the table as a force for good in your family's future. You may have some difficult or negative incidents in your past experiences around your table, but they don't have to keep you from the mealtime opportunities that lie ahead.

Our brokenness is often revealed at the dining table in a much more candid way than ever takes place in any counseling session or rehabilitation facility.

John Trent recalls, "During counseling with couples, we normally met at my office for the first few sessions. Eventually, I got to the place where I would do one session at their house. When you sit around the table at someone's home, it creates an entirely different atmosphere than in a church or a counseling room. You get an entirely different perspective when you visit in someone's home."[41]

To reclaim your table, begin by acknowledging that we have forgotten some elements in our busy culture. What used to be natural must now be intentional.

We need to go back and say, "This is why this mattered."

During my childhood, my mom had a Christmas season tradition of making tea rings, a potato-based bread ring pastry covered with sweet, delicious icing. She made extras on purpose so we could take some to our neighbors who might not have many special treats for Christmas. On Christmas Eve, we picked out three or four families who may have had a rough year, and we delivered the treats to the families.

We often encountered some special moments during those visits around the table. For instance, on one

Christmas Eve, we took a tea ring to a World War II veteran whose wife had just died. We delivered the treat and then sat with him as he poured out his heart in tears.

Mom's Tea Rings

The following recipe will make 3 tea rings.

Ingredients:

3 large potatoes
2 eggs
2/3 cup vegetable oil
1 package yeast
2/3 cup sugar
1 tsp salt
1 tsp milk
1 cup confectioners' sugar
1/2 tsp vanilla

Instructions:

1. Peel 3 large potatoes and boil until soft enough to mash. Drain but save the potato water. (You'll need it to mix with the yeast.) Mash the potatoes without adding anything.
2. In one bowl, mix together 2 eggs, 1 cup mashed potatoes, and 2/3 cup vegetable oil.

3. Mix the following in another bowl: 1 1/2 cups potato water (it needs to be warm), 1 package yeast, 2/3 cup sugar, 1 tsp salt.

4. Mix the contents of the two bowls together in a large bowl and add approximately 7 cups of flour. You'll know when you have enough or if you need to add more!

5. Knead (this is fun) until it is smooth and elastic, about 5 minutes. Roll into a ball and place in an oiled bowl. Cover with a paper towel or a tea towel and let it rest in a warm place for about 1.5 hours. To test for rising, stick two fingers in the dough. If holes are smooth, the dough is ready. Punch it down.

6. Roll the dough on a slightly floured countertop or board into a rectangle approximately 15 x 9 inches. Spread with melted butter.

7. Sprinkle the dough with sugar, cinnamon, and chopped pecans. Roll tightly, beginning at the wide side. Seal well by pinching the ends of the roll together.

8. Place the sealed side down on a lightly greased cookie sheet. Join the ends of the ring and seal. With scissors or a sharp knife, make cuts 2/3 of the way through the rings at about 1-inch intervals, turning each section on its side as you cut it. Put a pecan half in the center of each ring. Cover and let it rise another 30-45 minutes.

9. Bake at 345 degrees for about 15 minutes or until golden brown. Remove from the oven and brush the tops with melted butter.

10. Decorate by drizzling with a creamy white glaze: 1 teaspoon water or milk, 1 cup confectioner's sugar, and 1/2 teaspoon vanilla. Mix until smooth. Add holly and berries to decorate using red and green maraschino cherries and icing.

Those acts of kindness involving food left an indelible impression on me, creating a desire within me to want to do something special for people in need and causing me to hope that our children would catch on to that model. Today, you may not make tea rings, but you could do something similar by taking groceries to a family in need. Serving and doing something meaningful for someone else can be a way to reclaim a legacy that began long ago at your table.

The Empty Chair at the Table

What can you do when somebody is missing at the table or when you are suddenly eating alone? That is what Cherie Risinger experienced.

Cherie and Colin Risinger and their two children were a wonderful example to many at our church of how to be intentional in family life. They enjoyed regular meals together, used those occasions for "Faith Talks" with their kiddos, and even welcomed others to those mealtimes on occasion. Cherie and Colin had been married for eight-and-a-half years when Colin suddenly fell ill. He had previously suffered from an unusual autoimmune disorder called ITP, affecting his blood platelets and the blood's ability to clot, but this was different.

Colin had been in good health, feeling fine, and even training for a marathon. He hadn't been sick in months. But then he woke up on a Saturday morning and his eyes were yellow and possibly jaundiced. The next day he grew worse, nauseated and weak. Cherie took him to the hospital, and doctors discovered that Colin's own body was attacking his red blood cells, which ordinarily carried oxygen throughout his body, and his liver was not able to keep up.

The doctors gave him multiple blood transfusions but they could not get ahead of the disorder, and within a week, Colin's bodily organs all began shutting down. He had gone in to the hospital on Sunday, and the following Sunday, he was in heaven.

I got the word that Colin was in trouble during a Sunday morning service at Kingsland. I concluded the service and raced to the hospital to be with the family, and then went back to Kingsland in time to preach in the second service. By that time, others from Kingsland were already arriving to be with Cherie.

Colin and Cherie were quite active as greeters at Kingsland and had also been involved with their small group at church. Since the group was made up of younger couples, they were not accustomed to having a spouse pass away. Everyone was shocked at the news. Nevertheless, these young families sprang into action.

The first Sunday after Colin's death, the small group gathered together to discuss how they could serve Cherie and her children—Colin Jr., their seven-year-old son, and Avery, their five-year-old daughter. The group surrounded the family with love and prayers, flooded them with food and basic groceries, did the housecleaning chores, and mowed the Risingers' lawn. "People were sending me toothpaste in the mail," Cherie recalls. "I finally had to say, 'Okay, guys, we don't need any more!'"

Ironically, Cherie and Colin first attended Kingsland the Sunday that the former pastor announced that he was leaving. So it was not the preaching or teaching that kept the Risingers at Kingsland. It was the community. Cherie had already become involved in a Bible study for moms before their family showed up that first Sunday. Once she and Colin tasted of the Kingsland community, they were hooked. They loved the various opportunities to connect with other people and to serve. They were glad, too, for the teaching and activities for the kids.

Even in the hospital, members of Colin and Cherie's community group and others from Kingsland were there. Doug and Lisa Rogers, a mentor couple, stayed at the hospital with Cherie; they brought pillows and blankets for family members sleeping in the waiting room. When Colin's condition sharply declined, Cherie had given Colin to the Lord. "I know he is Yours, Lord." It helped Cherie in knowing that God was in charge.

When Colin passed away, Cherie leaned on Susan Sowell, the director of our Freedom Ministries at Kingsland, to help her explain to Colin Jr. and Avery that Daddy had gone to heaven and they would see him again. The kids had known that Colin was in the hospital, but they had no idea that he would never come home. Susan helped Cherie to walk through communicating that information to the children.

The Kingsland community wrapped their arms around the family, helping with the funeral expenses and other unexpected medical bills that Cherie could not have anticipated. God provided the financial resources the family needed, and when Cherie was ready, a member of her community group offered her a job with flexible hours so she could work around the children's school schedule.

"If you ever need help paying the mortgage," one of our pastors told Cherie, "please just let us know." Others continued to help with household chores, and still others have anonymously sent gift cards to the family.

"I've seen real Christianity," Cherie said later. "This is the way God intended His church and community to function. It is not merely going to a class in a building. It is truly doing life together."

As an unexpectedly single mom, Cherie has stayed connected to the community group, even though most everyone in the group is married. "Through the community group, I've been able to see how God has provided for my family and me. Losing Colin has been really hard, but God has blessed us and taken care of us. He has provided money and food and so many practical things."

Cherie still has occasional bad days when she gets down or lonely. "When that happens," she says, "I send a text message to some of my friends in the community group and say, 'I'm having a really rough day,' and they will pray for me. Or one of them will say, 'I'm available right now if you want to talk.' That has been an invaluable support group for me.

"I know that God is a good God, but I'm still learning to trust Him and to know that He has a bigger plan, that He will do something good even with the pain of losing my husband and the father of our children. I don't want it to be for nothing."

Probably one of the most challenging and loneliest experiences anyone can go through in life is to lose a spouse at a young age. Meaningful mealtimes have been an important part of the healing process for Cherie and the children. In a recent email, Cherie shared,

Meals and the ministry through food have played a role my family's story. After Colin passed my community group gave to us in many ways, but one big way was they provided meals for the kids and I for 6 months after he passed. And then they provided meals or food since then anytime I have been needing help. So even though it wasn't necessarily a conversation at a meal, providing dinner for me had a big impact and helped me so much. It has brought about conversations with my kids about helping others in need and has given me chances to share with others about how people blessed us with food.

Some may think that sitting at the same table as a family now would be too painful for Cherie's family, as the memories of Colin's presence reminds them of what they have lost. On the contrary, sitting at the table, even with that empty chair, recalls a hundred moments of blessing they experienced before he went to heaven. And that's why Cherie has been determined to reclaim her table with her kids. In fact, those memories of time around the table with Colin are even more meaningful now as the Risinger children can cherish the memories they had with their dad and the key lessons he and Cherie taught them. So mealtimes in their home have been reclaimed in numerous ways: the table has reclaimed the hope that despair tried to steal; the table has reclaimed the memories that sorrow threatened to take away; and the table reclaimed the legacy that Colin's death did not steal.

Reclaiming Our Cities

Dr. Elmo Johnson, an African American pastor, has been reclaiming the legacy of his family table for decades in one of Houston's most challenging sections of town, the Fourth Ward. Elmo isn't just a great pastor; he's one of my best friends and prayer partners. Even more, Elmo is a role model to many pastors, including me. He has taken dead aim at a culture where a lot of the dads are missing, in prison, or dead. Where other people see nothing but hopelessness and destruction, Elmo Johnson sees individuals who can be saved and transformed. He sees a future father and mom, someone who can bring healing to the city.

Working in a tough, inner-city context, Elmo reminds his congregation and the city of Houston that the church is the center of the community. The church he attended as a child—Morningstar Baptist Church—had a bell in the bell tower. That church was the center of the community, and it wasn't unusual for crowds to gather under that bell tower for "dinner on the grounds." Everyone would bring their favorite dish to share. I can almost smell the aromas now! The sharing didn't end around the potluck specials, though; whenever there was a need, somebody rang the church bell. Those, of course, were simpler times, and Elmo's current ministry has been more complicated. Even so, he's brought those same values (and some of the food) to Houston.

"But in the inner city, we are ravaged by drugs," Elmo admits. "Crack cocaine took over early in the 1990s, creating a wake of shootings and killings every day. We had to serve the children by being a father to those kids who no longer had a daddy, bringing those kids to church. Eventually, the kids brought their parents. Today, the church is filled with children of those children."

Elmo's encouragement to families today is to "Ring the bell!" Whether in an inner-city environment or an affluent city such as Katy, Elmo advises, "Love the people inside the church, nurture them, but then send them out into the community to ring the bell where there are broken homes and broken individuals. Get out from behind the walls of the church and step into the community to help meet the physical needs and the spiritual needs of the people."

For a number of years, Kingsland members have been going to the Fourth Ward to serve alongside Pastor Johnson and his team. "The children need love," says Elmo. "They don't see love; they see drugs. They see violence and death, but they don't see much love. So when the parents and kids from Kingsland go into that community, the children there get a glimpse of love."

We joined Elmo in his practical approach by supplying food to families in need. "Usually when families come to the church, we need to have some food there for them," he says. "It is hard for them to see Jesus when their stomachs are aching with hunger. So we feed them first. It is a part of us showing love and being fathers to the fatherless."

The work that Elmo is doing may take different forms than what we are doing, but the goal is the same—to help heal the culture by healing the family. "God instituted the family," Elmo often reminds us. "Family is the key to reaching this generation and a key to spiritual revival."

During the heat of the racial tension across America in the summer of 2020, I interviewed Elmo for an online forum on race. I asked him, "How is it that you have such a kind heart, that you are not angry?"

He told me more of his story. "When I was growing up in Louisiana, my single mom married someone and left," he said. "So my grandmother raised me. With no man in the family, the church was central to our lives."

That became the place where Elmo rang the bell, where he had mentors in his life that pointed him in the right direction. He developed a strong work ethic as well as an attitude that he did not have to be bitter, resentful, or hateful.

His grandmother raised him and poured into his life. She took Elmo to church and spoke freely about God around the family table. In a sense, to this day, he operates out of a spiritual understanding and a legacy that he inherited from her. Elmo looks back with fondness at the care of the church community that poured into him and met his family's physical needs as well. He reclaimed the values of his grandma. Some of the dishes he enjoys the most have to do with a "making the best of what you have" attitude that he saw modeled in his grandma, and he pulled those traits into a tough environment to help impact the next generation.

Red Beans and Rice

Ingredients:

1 lb. dry red beans

2 tbsp cooking oil

14 oz. andouille sausage

1 yellow onion

1 green bell pepper

3 ribs celery

4 cloves garlic

2 tsp smoked paprika

1 tsp dried oregano

1 tsp dried thyme

1/2 tsp garlic powder

1/2 tsp onion powder

1/4 tsp cayenne pepper

1/4 tsp freshly cracked black pepper

2 bay leaves

9 cups water, divided

1/4 cup chopped parsley

1 tbsp salt, or to taste

1 1/2 cups long grain white rice (uncooked)

3 green onions

Instructions:

1. Place the dry beans in a large bowl with double their volume of water and place them in the refrigerator. Allow the beans to soak overnight.

2. When it's time to cook, slice the sausage into rounds.

3. Add cooking oil and sliced sausage to a large pot and brown over medium heat.

4. While the sausage is cooking, dice the onion, bell pepper, and celery. Mince the garlic.

5. Remove the cooked sausage with a slotted spoon and place it in a bowl.

6. After the cooked sausage is removed, add the onion, bell pepper, celery, and garlic to the pot. Sauté over medium heat until the onions are soft. Those vegetables will pick up some of the brown bits off the bottom of the pot as you stir.

7. Add the smoked paprika, oregano, thyme, garlic powder, onion powder, cayenne, black pepper, and bay leaves to the pot. Stir and cook for another minute.

8. Drain and rinse the beans that have soaked overnight. Add 6 cups of water along with the beans to the pot. Stir the pot to combine the ingredients.

9. Turn the heat up to medium-high and place a lid on the pot. Bring it up to a boil. Once the pot is boiling, turn the heat down to medium-low. Let the pot cook at a low boil for an hour. Stir occasionally, but replace the lid after every stir.

10. After an hour, the beans should be tender. Begin smashing the beans with the back of a spoon against the side of the pot. Continue doing so with no lid as the pot simmers for another 30 minutes.

11. While the beans are simmering, cook the rice. Place rice and 3 cups water in a sauce pot. Turn the heat to high, place a lid on the pot, and bring it up to a boil. Once boiling, turn the heat down and let the rice simmer for 15 minutes. Afterward, turn the heat off and let the rice rest for 5 minutes without removing the lid.

12. Once the red beans have thickened, add the cooked sausage back to the pot. Add 1/4 cup chopped fresh parsley. Stir to combine. Taste the red beans and add salt according to your preferences.

13. Enjoy!

Today, Elmo Johnson is living out the legacy in Houston's Fourth Ward that he brought with him from Louisiana: living out the gospel, sharing meals, building relationships, and investing in—and changing—future generations. He has set the table in a really dark place and the walls have come down. His motto is, "If you want the world to come, ring the bell." The church bell? Oh, yes, and also the dinner bell.

The first time I went to see Elmo's inner-city church, he wanted to take me to lunch. "Okay," I said. "Take me to your favorite place."

Dr. Johnson eyed me curiously. "Are you sure that's where you want to go?" he asked, raising his eyebrows.

"Yes, absolutely," I replied. "I want to eat where you like to eat."

Dr. Johnson smiled and said, "Okay, you got it. This is it."

"What?"

He took me to lunch in Houston's Third Ward, a neighborhood nearby his own. We went to his favorite place called "This Is It," a locally popular "soul food" restaurant.

The name works well for locals, and everyone seems to know about it. "Where are we going to eat?"

"This is it."

That's all you need to know.

As a soul food restaurant, the menu at "This Is It" boasts such items as turnip greens, chitterlings, and oxtail.

"Have you ever had oxtail?" Dr. Johnson asked.

Now, I have spent most of my life in the southern portions of the United States, so I've enjoyed all sorts of special dishes, but oxtail?

"No, I don't think I have," I answered, wondering the same thing that is probably going through your mind right now. It is literally the cow's tail, which in decades past was often the only part of the cow that poor people could afford at the butcher shop. As a result, some enterprising cooks transformed it into a delicacy. It looks like a long, greasy hunk of fat and bony meat, boiled and covered in gravy.

"Well, you gotta try the oxtail," Dr. Johnson said, his eyes twinkling.

"Okay," I said. I took a big bite. I had never before eaten anything like oxtail, but if you really want to stretch your boundaries, sometimes you have to taste some things that you've never tried before. I'm not certain words can describe it; you just have to taste it yourself. But I ate the whole thing, and Elmo smiled at me the entire time! What did it taste like? Well, I'll just say it is an acquired taste. Having been there several times and enjoyed many delicious meals at "This Is It," I'd have to say the pepper steak is the winner, hands down.

While we were there, one of the servers, a young man, came up to Dr. Johnson. "Pastor Elmo," he said. "How are you, Brother Elmo?"

"I'm fine, son," Elmo said, as he dabbed his face with his napkin. "How are you doing?"

"I just got out of prison, and I got a job here," the young man said, his face beaming with pride.

"Oh, that's so good," Elmo said, getting up from the table and embracing the server. "I'm so proud of you. You are doing so well." Elmo didn't treat the young man as a former inmate; he didn't treat him as a server; no, Elmo treated the young man as his son.

A little while later, two women spotted us eating our turnip greens and oxtails and came to the table to greet Dr. Johnson. He got to his feet again and greeted the women, engaging them in conversation. "How are you doing?" he wanted to know. They talked briefly about some of their needs.

Elmo said, "Hold on just a second." He went outside and opened the trunk of his car. He came back in carrying two backpacks filled with school supplies. He handed the backpacks to the women. "Here, these are for you," he said.

The women's eyes filled with tears as they hugged the pastor. Clearly, the table at "This Is It" was a safe haven and facilitated talking about the brokenness in people's lives. Elmo has given me new eyes to see many things, not only about racial relationships but about every person's need for a relationship with Jesus, and those revelations have often begun with a meal and some food I had never before experienced.

Imagine what God might do in the lives of your family members and the lives of those in your community as you reclaim the legacy of your mealtimes. He may affect your future family tree as you turn your table into a safe haven where a person can find nourishment not only for the physical body but for the soul as well.

CHAPTER 6

A Table Redeemed

The table is not only a place for renewed connection. It is also a place of redemption. In Scripture, the word *redemption* basically involves God purchasing back something that has been lost. You may have lost a relationship or a career or have otherwise experienced deep pain in your life, but you can go back to the table and find redemption as you allow God to bring good out of those situations. He wants to renew, replace, or restore what you lost in those prior experiences.

Keep in mind, you can't revive what isn't alive or was never alive. You can't restore what you never had in the first place. So if you have never had a relationship with Jesus, the place to start is by putting your trust in Him. He can pick up the broken pieces of your life and put you back together again, redeemed, purchased by God for His glory and your good.

You may be saying, "That sounds great, but I had a terribly messed up childhood. How can that be redeemed?"

God uses all of our experiences, the good and the bad, the enjoyable and the difficult, for His glory and our good, if we are willing to let Him do that. Brad Flurry discovered that truth as he made himself available to God. To me, Brad's story is the redeemed version of author J. D. Vance's best-selling book, *Hillbilly Elegy*, in which he describes how he overcame the poverty and trauma of his childhood in a rural, blue-collar family by escaping to the US Marine Corps. Vance went on to attend Yale Law School and became a lawyer. Brad did something equally as difficult: he served in the US Marines for nearly twenty years and then became a pastor.

As a child, Brad had endured an extremely dysfunctional home, but he accepted Christ at a church camp when he was only eight years of age. Brad recalls, "Our student pastor presented an old-fashioned fire-and-brimstone message, and I knew I didn't want to go to hell, so I stepped up and asked Jesus to save me."

Going back home after camp, however, exacerbated further the stark contrast between Brad's family and others.

In one of his last memories of interaction with his dad, Brad recalls that his dad came to pick him up along with his brother to take them for a special weekend together. Their dad checked them in at a Ramada Inn hotel and asked the boys, "What do you want to eat? I'll get it for you."

The boys requested some cereal, so their dad went out and bought some. When he returned to the hotel, he said, "Here's some cereal. I'll be back in a little while."

He left . . . and didn't come back for two days.

It was then that Brad realized, "My dad does not care about us."

To compensate for the dysfunction in his family, Brad spent a lot of time away from home and more time with his friends.

"I played sports and a lot of my friends' dads were believers in Jesus," Brad said. "They took me under their wings, even though I was not their son."

Brad recalls, "Scott Nash was my best friend. Scott's father, Troy, owned his own business, so he hired me to work on construction jobs with them during the summer."

As much as he appreciated the employment, Brad saw something even more valuable in his boss. "Day in and day out, I witnessed that man loving his family well," Brad said.

Even though there was chaos and confusion in my own home, I saw an example of what a family could be by watching how the Nash family worked.

I ate many meals with them in their home. They included me at their table as part of their family, and in many ways, they influenced my life forever. I often stayed at their home overnight on Saturday and went to church with them on Sunday mornings. Even though I wasn't their son, they took me under their wing.

Troy Nash, Scott's dad, was a coach and a Sunday school teacher, and he was a great dad. He blessed his kids. He spoke into their lives. He was an active participant in his kids' lives. He was there for his kids, not just at every event but at every practice. Some parents think that simply being in the same house is all that is necessary to make a positive impact on their kids' lives. But proximity doesn't equal presence. Troy Nash seemed to know that, so I saw Troy Nash model sacrificial parenting, loving his family well.

It is okay to remember what you never had. That's where the brokenness piece comes in, but don't stop there. Allow the Lord to redeem what hurt you, what the Enemy used in his attempts to destroy you. You can't do that on your own, but God can redeem your situation.

The Greatest Man I Never Knew

My good friend John Trent has helped to strengthen thousands of families over the years through his insightful writings, and he has a story very similar to Brad's.

With his two brothers, one of whom, Jeff, was his twin, John lived with their single mom. As John tells it,

> Jeff and I were playing in a regional football game, in the regional finals. My twin brother and I were in the same backfield.
>
> The *Arizona Republic*, the biggest newspaper in the area, did a story about Jeff and me, and somehow our dad saw the article and called our mom. He said that he was going to come to our game. Our dad had left our family when Jeff and I were two months old, and we had never met him. Throughout our upbringing, he lived barely twenty miles away, but he had no contact with us. Now, suddenly, because we had been featured in the newspaper, he promised that he was going to come to our big game.
>
> Jeff and I played our hearts out, watching for him throughout the game.
>
> But our dad never showed up.
>
> Mom was there. But Dad was drunk someplace.
>
> The game was over. . . . We got on the bus and left, without ever seeing our dad. We realized that Dad could care less about us.[42]

Just as the Nash family mealtime made a difference in Brad's Flurry's life, John experienced something similar with Doug Darren, his Young Life leader. One day, to thank him, John put his lawn mower in his old Volkswagen van and drove over to Doug's house to cut the Young Life leader's grass.

"What are you doing here, John?" Doug asked when he heard the lawn mower's motor and stepped outside the house to see who was mowing his lawn.

"Oh, I was in the area with my mower," John said, "so I thought I'd stop by and cut your grass."

"I'll give you some money," Doug said.

"No, no," John said. "I don't want any money," even though he desperately needed it.

"Well, would you like to come in to eat with us?" Doug asked.

"Okay," John said. "Yeah, I would like to do that."

For the first time in his life, John sat down at a dinner table where the family held hands and thanked God for His blessings. Doug and his wife had a four-year-old and a six-year-old, so it wasn't a fancy meal. But it was a family around the table. It was the first time that John saw a dad lead his family in prayer and bless them. And it changed John Trent's life. John has gone on to be a blessing to millions of other families, including mine and many families in our church, but the influence God gave him started right there around the table.

There may have been pain at your table. Maybe you recall experiences such as Brad's cereal at the Ramada Inn, or John's dad who never showed up. But God redeemed those situations in both of those men's lives. If you had similar pain in your life, you, too, can go back to the table and find redemption, when God purchases back something that has been lost. You may have suffered loss, but God can use even that in your life and in your family members' lives.

It is impossible to get past the emotional wounds, hurt, and pain in life until we acknowledge them. Suppressing those things doesn't help; covering them over with external facades only allows the wounds to fester and get worse. We can't circumvent the pain; we have to go through it if we are ever going to get beyond it.

I realized that as a husband and a father, as well as a pastor, the process would probably have to start with me. Through the years, I've grown more willing to admit from the platform my personal failures and struggles, not as a public confessional or as a "poor, poor, pitiful me" expression, but in hopes that people who hear me will understand that regardless of our position in life, we all struggle, and we're all carrying a heavy load. As I've grown older and more experienced in ministry, I've realized that people are less interested in how polished I am and are far more interested in those times when our family has struggled with real-life situations, even where we've made a mess of things. They want to know what we have learned from those situations or what we would change if we could. As a result, in situations where I used to share "success stories," I'm far more open to sharing the hard parts of our story, especially the pieces of the puzzle that don't seem to fit perfectly. Slowly, this has generated more openness in the church, and people have caught on to the idea that it is okay to say, "I'm not okay."

Truth is, most people identify more with our failures than our successes, so when you acknowledge your brokenness, I believe you are inviting people to connect in a deeper way. We all struggle, and everyone you meet is dealing with some difficulty, whether this is apparent or not.

Every one of us has a table story. Some of us have eaten around a "crazy" table, a "scary" table, a "lonely" table, an "empty" table, or maybe you have eaten at a legacy table that has otherwise profoundly affected your life. Regardless of what you have experienced in the past around your tables, God can redeem those things and use them to strengthen you and your family in the future.

Many people have stories of redemption, stories of going through the flood or the fire and finding the good that came out of it. I've mentioned the meal Jesus shared with some of His disciples in John 21, after His resurrection. Jesus prepared a meal of fish on the banks of the Sea of Galilee as the sun was coming up. There may be no better example of a time when food and redemption came together. Remember, Peter had denied his Lord the night before Christ was crucified. Then he returned to what he knew before he'd followed Jesus: he was fishing at night. Theologians have debated through the years whether Peter was fishing because he had forsaken his calling or because he was waiting on his next instructions from God, but it seems to me that Peter had gone off mission and was back to his old way of life. Either way, we can tell by his reaction that this situation became a turning point. He'd fished all night only to come back to shore with empty nets. That experience must have brought back memories of another such futile night, recorded in Luke 5. In that instance, he had returned to shore, was instructed by Jesus to throw his nets out one more time, and experienced the greatest catch of his life.[43] In this case, the same thing happened. And when it did, Peter knew right away who was calling out to him from shore. He didn't event wait for the boat to come in; Peter jumped into the water and swam to Jesus. What happened next was pivotal.

Jesus was cooking fish over a fire of coals. This sort of fire is described in only two places in Scripture: during this encounter in John 21 and in John 18:18, where, as Peter was warming himself over a fire of coals, he adamantly denied knowing Jesus. Imagine the memories, shame, and regret that came flooding back as the smells took him back to that fateful moment. He stood again over a similar fire as the risen Jesus restored him. It was as though, even through the preparation of a meal, Jesus was saying, "I want to take you back to the darkest place in your life, because I want to redeem your story as we share this breakfast together."

That's what Jesus came to earth to do: redeem stories of those who are far from God, who feel that they're too far gone and yet deeply desire to respond to His voice. I can think of no better invitation to accept. If you have never accepted the grace that God offers through Jesus, I pray that you would now.

*   *   *   *   *

The moment Lana and I walked into the home of Todd and Lorie Pendergrass and their four-year-old son, Hudson, the sweet aroma of the prepared dinner greeted and surrounded us. It was a meal that evoked special memories for all of us—chicken pot pie, a family recipe of Lorie's. It is a relatively easy recipe but it is especially delicious because Lorie puts cranberry sauce right on top of the pot pie after she cooks it. Prior to enjoying Lorie's specialty, I had never before eaten cranberry sauce with chicken pot pie, but now I love it and can't imagine how bland pot pie might be without it.

Sitting around the kitchen table with Todd and Lorie, it was difficult to keep our emotions under control. Lana and I were sharing our first meal with Todd and Lorie since they were back in their home together after a devastating house fire. We were overflowing with joy because they had made it through the fire that had gutted their kitchen and ruined their home with smoke and water damage.

But our emotions were stirred by more than simply the physical restoration of their home. It was deeply meaningful to all four of us that we were at the Pendergrass home for dinner. After the house had been repaired, after all the smoke and water damage had been cleared, we sat down at a restored kitchen table, a new table, and we all sensed that the table was a picture of their lives. We understood that the fire was symbolic of the past twenty years in Todd and Lorie's lives, and the new table was symbolic of God's redemption of what seemed to be a hopeless story.

Todd Pendergrass had accepted the position at Kingsland as the executive pastor of administration on August 13, 2017, and he and Lorie and their family had moved into their home only six days later. Just a month earlier, Lorie and Todd had been looking for a place to live in Nashville. In June 2017 they were close to making a decision on a home when a church staffing organization we were working with called Todd on a Thursday. He had not applied with them and hadn't had any serious dealings with them since 2012, but the representative said, "We have a church in Texas that is interested in you and we need to give them an answer on Monday. We ran across your résumé in our files and wondered if you would pray about allowing us to submit your name."

"Well, sure, but I don't have to pray about that. I'm open to the possibilities, so just submit my name. What church is it and where?"

"Kingsland Baptist Church in Katy, Texas."

"Is that a Southern Baptist Church?" Todd asked.

"Yes, it is."

"Do they know that I have been divorced and have remarried?" Todd asked.

"Yes," the representative replied. "But they say that doesn't disqualify you."

"Oh, I think it probably will," Todd answered. As a former Southern Baptist preacher, he knew the long-standing views on divorce held by most Southern Baptist churches.

Todd had worked hard and was pouring his life into a successful ministry when his marriage fell apart. When he and his former wife divorced, it not only devastated his family but Todd lost his ministry and everything else that was meaningful to him. He thought his life was over and that he'd never be back in pastoral ministry.

An important side note: What Todd did not know was that we had already been grappling with those issues and having productive discussions about divorced people at Kingsland for some time. A couple of years before the opportunity to bring Todd on our team, I saw the challenging topic of divorce as an opportunity for teaching and change at Kingsland—not because we wanted to "soften our views for the times" but because I was convinced the Scriptures provided a way forward for those in leadership who had walked this difficult road. Similar to many churches, Kingsland had a history of opposition to having divorced men serve as deacons, much less pastors on our staff. A group of key leaders among our deacons joined me in taking an in-depth look at the topic of divorce in the Bible and came away with the same conclusions. As heartbreaking and devastating as divorce could be to people and their families, we serve a God who has the power to redeem the toughest of circumstances!

So as it became more apparent that Todd was the right man to join the staff at Kingsland, I knew that there would be some who saw it as a bad idea—even one that they perceived to be forbidden in Scripture. I realized there could be "easier hires" without the hassle, but I also knew God was leading me to take the harder road—not only for Todd's sake but on behalf of anyone who ever felt left behind, missing out on the full impact of redemption.

I decided to present a strategic plan. I prepared a two-page document for our personnel committee outlining my biblically based views on divorce. I emphasized that in marriage, "one man and one woman for life" is the ideal biblical pattern, but we live in a broken world. Certainly, in the Old Testament, God straightforwardly declared through the prophet Malachi, "I hate divorce."[44] Jesus acknowledged that it was because of men's hardness of heart that Moses permitted divorce, but divorce was not God's original intention. Nevertheless, Jesus seemed to permit it when adultery was involved.[45] The apostle Paul added to that in 1 Corinthians 7, describing situations of abandonment; if an unbeliever wants to leave, let him (or her) leave. Certainly, a relationship in which domestic abuse occurs has already broken the covenantal vows of marriage, so for any of those three reasons—adultery, abandonment, or abuse—divorce made sense to me.

The personnel committee and I sat around the table and thoroughly discussed the issues. The committee decided to ask Todd to come for an interview. Lorie and Todd traveled to Katy to meet with the personnel committee as well as Brad Flurry and me.

By the time we finished our get-together, there was no doubt that Todd and Lorie were meant to be part of our team. The committee unanimously recommended him and Kingsland welcomed Todd and his family with open arms.

Todd and Lorie fit perfectly with the other staff members and wives. Over the next fifteen months, Todd and Brad Flurry got busy. They were a tremendous complement to each other, taking much of the administration of Kingsland off my shoulders. As we were immersed in celebrating the 2018 Christmas season, Brad and his wife, Liz; Lana and I; and Todd and Lorie each hosted a fantastic, progressive Christmas party in our homes for all of our staff members and wives, about 125 people.

The evening of Thursday, December 13, everyone gathered at the church and pulled a card out of a basket. The card indicated which of the three homes where they were to have dinner—at the Flurrys', the Pendergrass's, or the Ryans'. Following dinner, everyone was to gather at another large home, one that could accommodate the entire group for dessert.

Lorie and Todd's home was decorated exquisitely for Christmas, replete with their Christmas tree, pine garlands, outdoor lighting, and numerous Christmas candles throughout the house. More than twenty-five people gathered at Todd and Lorie's home for dinner. Todd took off his sports coat and hung it up in the laundry room where both he and Lorie donned long, white restaurant-style aprons as they served the food.

Everyone enjoyed a delicious meal, and then at 7:30 p.m. they were to leave Todd and Lorie's to travel the short distance to join the larger gathering for dessert. Shortly before the guests left their home, Lorie left to go help prepare for the larger group. "Make sure you blow out all the candles," she called to Todd, who stayed behind to close up the house after all the guests had departed.

"Okay, I will," Todd assured her.

After the last guests were on their way, Todd walked throughout the house extinguishing the many decorative Christmas candles. When he was done, he went back to the laundry room to get his jacket. He removed his apron and tossed it on a counter in the laundry room, where their tea and coffee urns and other party food items were located.

Todd pulled the laundry room door shut behind him and headed to the dessert venue, about a mile away. The house was filled with a joyous Christmas spirit, and as Todd walked in, he immediately began greeting other staff and friends in the kitchen. With more than 125 people there, the noise level was loud and enthusiastic.

Meanwhile, Todd and Lorie's babysitter for the evening, Tammy, a schoolteacher from Kingsland, returned to their home with Hudson to put him to bed. As Tammy and Hudson walked up the driveway toward the house, they heard a loud popping noise. The wind was blowing, so Tammy didn't think much of it. They continued up the left side of the house, toward the back gate, where they heard another cracking sound. As they reached the back of the house and turned toward the door, they saw a bright, flickering light through the kitchen window. They looked inside and saw flames coming out of the laundry room into the kitchen.

Both Hudson and Tammy saw the fire at the same time, so Tammy, the quintessential calm, collected schoolteacher said, "Well, Hudson, it looks like the house is on fire. Let's walk back to the car." As they walked, Tammy called 911 to report the fire. Once in the car, she remained calm and tried to prepare Hudson. "We're going to pull down the street a bit, and in just a minute, you're going to see fire trucks come by here. They're going to help at your house."

"Well, I've seen fire trucks before," Hudson replied. "I don't want to see any fire trucks."

When the firemen arrived, they had difficulty getting through the front door and finally had to ramrod it to break into the home.

Tammy, in the meantime, was calling Lorie at the party, but Lorie had laid her phone on a counter and didn't see it. Just then, Todd walked by the counter and noticed that Lorie's phone showed a missed call from Tammy. Todd picked up the phone and waved it to his wife. "You've missed a call from Tammy!" he called across the noisy, crowded kitchen.

Lorie recalls, "My first thought was, 'Oh, goodness! What has Hudson done that Tammy has to call me about it?'"

She dialed Tammy's number, and when Tammy picked up, Lorie said, "Oh, girl! I hope that he is behaving himself!"

In her calm voice, Tammy flatly said, "Lorie, your house is on fire."

"Oh, Tammy! You are so funny!" Lorie said, thinking that Tammy was joking with her.

Tammy repeated the message several times before Lorie realized that she was serious. When the message sunk in to her, she yelled back to Tammy, "Our dog! Our dog is in the house." Their tiny toy poodle, Lacy, was inside the house.

"Lorie, I can't get your dog," Tammy said, still composed. "Your house is on fire."

In the midst of the Christmas festivities, Lorie screamed across the kitchen to Todd, "Our house is on fire!"

Todd thought she meant that a cooktop or something was still burning. But Lorie was still yelling.

Terry Sowell was standing next to Todd in the kitchen. He grabbed Todd's arm and said, "Let's go!" They pushed through the crowded house and out the front door. The moment they stepped outside, they heard the sirens.

"Terry, they're going to my house," Todd said.

"Yeah, I know."

When they arrived at the house, eleven emergency vehicles were already there. Todd got out of the car and ran up the sidewalk toward the house, intent on rescuing Lacy. A fireman stopped him. "You can't go in there," he said. "It's too dangerous."

"We have a dog in there," Todd said.

"Where would the dog be?"

"Probably in the master bedroom, under the bed. That's where she hides when she is afraid."

The fireman nodded and headed into the fire. In less than a minute, he returned, carrying Lacy. He handed the soot-covered poodle to Todd and went back inside the burning house.

By now Lorie, Brad and Liz Flurry, and a number of the Kingsland staff members—Lana, Susan Sowell, Judi Post and her husband, Dan—and I were there at the house too. Todd later said, "I kept thinking, I don't have any idea what I'm supposed to do right now." There was nothing anyone could do but watch and pray that the house could be saved. The women gathered in a circle praying, and the guys gathered in a separate circle, asking God to intervene and praying for Lorie and Todd.

Interestingly, when we looked up from our prayer, a group of firemen had come out of the house and were lined up by their trucks, watching us pray.

As everyone continued looking on, watching the firemen make sure all the flames and hotspots were out, Brad and I nudged closer to Todd and Lorie. "You're not going to go through this by yourselves," I said, placing my hand on Todd's shoulder.

"There will be $5,000 put in your bank account tonight," Brad said. "Your computer that was burnt up in the fire will be replaced first thing tomorrow morning."

"You have your choice from plenty of places you can stay," I told Todd and Lorie. "You just have to decide where you want to stay." Already, before the fire was even extinguished, we'd had more than a dozen offers, including Terry and Susan's home, where Todd and Lorie and Hudson had lived for nine days following Hurricane Harvey.

"We'll just go back to Terry and Susan's house," Todd and Lorie said. They were comfortable there, and Terry and Susan had said they'd gladly open their home again to the family that night.

When the firemen were certain that the fire was completely extinguished, the fire chief led Todd and Lorie and our Kingsland group into the home. A sickening, foul-smelling smoke still wafted through every room. Everything in the house was ruined by the fire, water, or smoke.

"Tell me what you think happened," the chief said to Todd.

"I'm pretty sure that the fire started because I threw my apron in the laundry room," Todd told him, taking responsibility for the accident. "I didn't remember the candle burning on the counter, and I'm sure that apron landed on or near the candle."

"Do you think there was any foul play?" the fire chief asked.

"No, I'm fairly certain the apron caught on fire."

Walking through the house, we knew that it would have to be gutted. The smoke and soot covered everything, even upstairs, all the way to the attic. The ventilation system had been on, so it had pumped the smoke throughout the dwelling. Every piece of furniture, every stitch of clothing, everything would have to be cleaned or replaced from top to bottom. Few things in life are more overwhelming than a house fire.

Dan and Judi Post had left the fire scene earlier without Todd or Lorie's knowledge. The Posts went to a department store and purchased several bags full of basic essentials, things such as clothes, toothbrushes, and other things. They took the items to the Sowells' home and left the bags on the front porch. When the Pendergrass family arrived at the Sowells' home around midnight, they were surprised to see the gifts waiting for them.

The night of the fire, Todd and Lorie had left some wrapped Christmas presents under the Christmas tree. They had planned to take the presents to Alabama on December 16 to celebrate Christmas with their extended family members. To everyone's amazement, the presents survived the fire, but they had been doused by water and were covered with heavy smoke and soot.

Despite the devastating fire, Todd and Lorie decided to go ahead with their trip to Alabama, partly just to let their family members know that they were okay. Before they left, however, several people from the church gathered together at the Pendergrass home and retrieved the Christmas presents that had been underneath the tree. They peeled the crud off each present, cleaned them all, and then rewrapped them so Lorie and Todd could take the presents to their family.

Nobody said to Todd or Lorie, "Just call us if there is anything we can do." Nobody called and asked, "Do you need anything?"

No, the people of Kingsland just jumped in and did it. J. P. and Jessie Pruett, still reeling from their own devastating losses from Hurricane Harvey, went out and bought toys for Hudson that same night as the fire. "We knew that Hudson's toys and Christmas presents had all been destroyed by the fire," Jessie said later, "so we wanted him to have some things to play with." But the couple did not merely purchase new toys for Hudson. They didn't merely purchase toys they thought Hudson might enjoy. In an intentional effort, they went to stores and bought toys they knew Hudson had *before* the fire, and replaced them. As much as possible, they bought new versions of the toys that Hudson had lost in the fire. It was God's way of showing Hudson He cared for him, and He could redeem any situation and restore to him what he had lost, even as a little boy.

On their way back from Alabama, Todd talked with Brad Flurry by phone. "Don't worry," Brad said, "by the time you get back here, we're going to have a good place for you to live till your house is ready."

Todd continued driving toward Katy, not knowing exactly where they would go once they arrived back home. Along the way, Brad called and gave Todd an address where they were to go that night to stay. A family had invited the Pendergrass family to live without cost in their beautiful home for months while they were working for Exxon in Alaska.

When Lorie, Todd, and Hudson walked into the house that night, they were shocked. Lana and Liz had gone into the burned-out home and had retrieved the family's Christmas stockings that had been hanging on the fireplace mantle. They had washed the stockings, filled them with goodies, and hung them in the family's home away from home. They had also set up two Christmas trees and decorated them. On one of the trees were pictures of the Pendergrass family. They had tried to make everything look as close to home as possible.

For the next seven months, the people of Kingsland wrapped their arms around Lorie and Todd and the family. The strong friendships that came out of that time shaped all of us and caused us to be a little more like Jesus.

As we sat around their kitchen table in their cleaned, freshly painted, and renewed home, the stress of the flood and fire they had endured was a metaphor for their lives. Yes, they had suffered loss; they had endured a great deal of pain. But God brought them through the literal fire of their home and the relational fire of severed marriages. And around this new table, we celebrated the redemption of both home and family. We enjoyed Lorie's special pot pie—along with the cranberries—and we celebrated God's goodness in their lives and His love and power to redeem even difficult situations, to restore hope in all of our lives.

Lorie's Easy Chicken Pot Pie Recipe

Ingredients:

1 package of 2 ready-made double pie crusts

1 15-ounce can "Veg-All" mixed vegetables (drained)

1 10.5-ounce can of cream of potato soup

1 10.5-ounce can of cream of chicken soup

1/4 cup milk

3 cups of precooked chicken

1/4 tsp poultry seasoning

1 can of cranberry sauce

Instructions:

1. Preheat oven to 350 degrees.

2. Mix the drained vegetables, potato soup, cream of chicken soup, and milk in a bowl. Add in the chopped or shredded chicken and stir.

3. Fill the bottom of a deep-dish pie plate with one crust. Pour in the contents and stir.

4. Top the pie with the other crust and crimp around the edges. (After this, Lorie brushes the crust with an egg wash.) Place slits in center of pie with a knife.

5. Wrap foil around the edges of the crusts to keep them from browning too quickly. Bake for 40 to 50 minutes. Remove from the oven and let sit for 10 minutes.

6. Slice or spoon, and serve with the cranberry sauce.

(Adapted from Soulfully Made[46])

CHAPTER 7

The Resting Table

The truth is, the family table is often a good barometer of how restless we are—eating a steady diet of fast food, eating in front of the television, eating hurriedly in the car—and believe it or not, it probably says something about how we feel about God.

Why are we not having these meaningful mealtimes with our families?

We're too busy.

Why are we not enjoying quality time with our heavenly Father?

We're too restless.

The table says a lot about you.

Understandably, the "habit of rest" may sound foreign to some people. We *are* all so busy. We're running with work; with school activities, including academics;

with sports, artistic, and dramatic practices; and with other events. *Rest?* What is that?

The rest we are talking about flows out of God's grace, His love and favor that He freely gives to us. If we really understand that God loves us, we can relax and rest in His presence. This sort of rest is more about being in the presence of the Father than the amount of time we spend in church services, Bible reading, or even prayer.

The opposite is true as well. Persistent restlessness grows in the absence or misunderstanding of grace. If you are working, striving, and constantly trying to claw yourself into earning a place at God's table or deserving God's favor, you are going to be continually exhausted and frustrated—and you certainly will not find any meaningful rest.

Accepting that you already have a place at the table, rather than trying to earn it, is essential to understanding why you can rest in your heavenly Father's presence. Until you believe this, you won't be able to facilitate a similar environment for others. Some of us never felt deserving at our tables growing up, so we've been trying to earn our place ever since.

That attitude kept one of my good friends, Gil Harris, away from God's table, even though he was in close proximity for years. Gil and his wife, Tracy, moved to Katy from Mobile, Alabama, in 1997 after serving in ministry for more than twenty years.

Throughout his childhood and early teen years, Gil had been the apple of his dad's eye. Much of his dad's approval, however, hinged on Gil's athletic ability. At least that's how Gil saw it. And who could blame him? The better he performed, the more his dad beamed with pride. Then Gil's dad developed Hodgkin's disease, and though he was physically in the room, he was no longer emotionally present with the family. No longer did he express approval of Gil or his siblings. He turned inward into his own pain. Around that same time, Gil's athletic career came to an end, primarily because of his slight build, further exacerbating the loss of his dad's approval.

Gil interpreted his dad's withholding of love as personal rejection. *It must be my fault. What did I do wrong? Why don't you like me anymore?* Gil fretted. *I need you; I want your attention; I want to know you, Dad, but you don't seem to care about me anymore.* Gil carried that emotional pain with him throughout his teenage years, all the way to his dad's death when Gil was eighteen.

Gil transferred that performance mentality and the resultant insecurity to his relationship with God. As an on-fire Christian, he threw himself into working harder in the ministry. *If I'm going to get God's attention, and earn a spot at His table, I have to perform well* he said to himself. Unfortunately, that led to spiritual burnout, and Gil left the ministry.

When Gil and Tracy visited Kingsland, they found a spiritual home for themselves and their four kids. They got busy and immersed themselves in the community. At the same time, Gil's new career—operating an auto repair business—prospered.

Yet, as they so often do, spiritual rule-keeping and addiction go hand in hand. Legalism and secret sins are strange but frequent bedfellows. Even while Gil continued to maintain the outward look of success to his peers, he grew to depend on alcohol to self-medicate each day. In time, Gil became a full-blown alcoholic, despite being deeply involved in church life. How could that happen? Could it be that when he turned to alcohol, Gil was trying to feed a hunger, attempting to compensate for a scarcity of time and acceptance around his teenage table?

In January 2010, Tracy looked at Gil and said, "Gil, we are going in two different directions, and I am not going to go in your direction."

He promised Tracy and himself that he would make some changes, attempting to improve himself, and for the next three months, he sincerely tried.

And failed.

Gil got more involved in the church and did his best to break his bad habits. After three months of abject failure, Gil experienced a total breakdown in the back office of his auto shop. "God, I can't do this," he cried, shaking his fists at God. "I've never been able to do this, so why don't You just kill me and take me out of here? Send me to hell or do whatever You want to do. Just take me out. I'm done."

What happened next surprised the former preacher. Gil said, "I heard God speak to me in a voice that was *louder* than an audible voice, and He said, 'It's about time. I thought you'd never give up. I've been waiting your whole life for you to give up and give in, and let Me take over.'"

Now, at last, Gil began to understand God's grace, that he didn't have to earn God's love or a place at His table. Gil said, "I felt God saying to me, 'There's nothing you have to do. I am absolutely crazy about you. I will change you along the way; just let Me do the changing.'"

This truth set Gil free—free to be the Christian he had always hoped to be as well as the husband and father Tracy and his kids needed him to be.

Nevertheless, his new relationship with God was not a quick fix. In fact, Gil continued to drink, even after his recommitment to the Lord. Knowing that there were other guys like him in our city, every third Thursday, Gil hosted an event at his auto shop that he called "Bar-B-Q, Beer, and Bible," an informal, "spirited" Bible study. It was as unchurchy as a Bible study could be as they gathered around physical food in search of spiritual food. It took two more years for Gil to get sober.

Not all of the guys responded positively to vulnerability, transparency, or to group discussions of personal issues, but Gil always took time to pray with the men. More than a few of them suffered from what Gil called "Dad deprivation"; they had never truly experienced the love of their father, and the feelings of insecurity, failure, and lack of acceptance—even in the lives of highly successful men—still haunted them.

Many came to Gil with tears in their eyes.

"Look, we have to deal with some of those things from our past," Gil told them. "We have to find forgiveness and acceptance. We need to be open and honest with God." Many of the men found freedom from the bondage that had held them for years. Others did not.

Gil remained undaunted. "When someone chose to walk away, I'd always pray for him. Sometimes when I complained to God about the guys who didn't get it, God would remind me, 'Well, it only took fifty-three years for Me to get ahold of you and for you to catch on!'"

Striving to be accepted by God had driven Gil to drinking and nearly destroyed his family. Discovering that he could rest and know that he was accepted at God's table changed Gil Harris forever.

Like Gil, many people have trouble resting in God's grace because of their past experiences. You may feel condemned because you could not live up to your earthly father's expectations or demands. For some, that starts when we are kids. "You got a B in that class. Why didn't you get an A?"

"You are playing second clarinet, but if you worked harder, you could be the first chair clarinetist."

"Why are you the sixth man on the basketball team instead of a starter?"

Do you really understand how God sees you? His perspective is completely different from what is commonly portrayed. So often God is presented as the angry Father who is never pleased with you—indeed, that you *cannot* please Him no matter how hard you try and no matter what you do.

But in truth, He is not that angry God waiting for you to get your stuff together. Instead, the image of God that Jesus described for us is the father of the prodigal son who is longing for his child to return, who runs to the wayward son when he sees him inching toward him and welcomes him home.

Is God the Creator of all universes? Yes. Is He the Judge before whom every person will one day give an account? Yes. But most of all, He is your loving heavenly Father—and no matter how badly you have messed up, what a difference it makes when the Judge is your kind, gracious, loving Father who is not seeking to punish you but rather is inviting you to discover who you were really born to be and restoring you to your position in His family! He is the Father who has redeemed you, who has bought back that which was lost and will welcome you around His family table.

Why is this important?

Because your concept of God will color not only what you think and believe but what you do, what you say, what matters to you, how you live, and how you treat everyone around you. Let's face it: Many of our misconceptions about God stem from what we experienced with our own fathers around the family table. You may have been the victim of harsh, condemning words or of a critical spirit expressed by your mother or father. Or perhaps your dad wasn't at the dinner table at all.

So many people—even those who seem fabulously successful in certain ways—still feel insecure or unfulfilled because they could never please mom or dad, or live up to someone else's expectations. We all have misconceptions about God that we have dragged along from our own relationships with our human father.

Growing up, I didn't see *rest* modeled well. My dad had grown up on a farm in Indiana, and hard work was part of his life. He worked all the time. His attitude was, "Put your feet on the floor and you will find something to do." Dad actually played college and professional basketball before serving our country honorably during the Vietnam War and earning a Silver Star. When he left the air force when I was five, he started a small airline, then developed a small airport, and owned several businesses along the way. He later worked for American Airlines, then became the president of the largest corporate aviation company in the United States.

Dad was a self-proclaimed workaholic until he developed heart disease. Prior to that, he worked all the time. The family meals I described previously didn't happen in the early years of my life, because my parents were working so many hours. If I wanted to hang out with my dad, I had to work. Truth is, Dad and I didn't often hang out together until he had the health issues. As a boy, I didn't do recreational stuff with my dad. We worked. While I'm thankful that my dad instilled within me a strong work ethic, when I attempted to take that same attitude into my spiritual life, I was setting myself up for failure.

By the time I was in seventh grade, our family renewed their commitment to Christ. Shortly after that, I was called to the ministry. As I studied the Scriptures, I realized that I needed to undo a lot of my thinking about resting in the Lord and how I could find acceptance with God. I discovered that it's not about what I do for Him, but it is about what He has done for me.

I'm probably not alone in my prior misconceptions. Many of us wear our "busyness" like a badge of honor. "Congratulations to *me*. I'm so busy. I worked till three last night." But stop and think about that: In what other area of life do we consider exhaustion a plus?

The principle of Sabbath rest goes all the way back to Genesis 2. God designed us to enjoy rest. In fact, such rest was never meant to be a burden, but a blessing! Jesus once said, "The Sabbath was made for man, not man for the Sabbath."[47] His point was that we were made to enjoy margin. It's no coincidence, by the way, that the traditional beginning of the Jewish Sabbath is marked by a family meal. The Sabbath even showed up in the Ten Commandments, and even though the New Testament makes it clear we're not bound to any particular day any longer, the idea that we were made for regular rest still stands. What other command of God do we violate so freely yet feel so good about it?

For some reason, we think it is okay to work ourselves into an early grave, all in the name of trying to please God. That doesn't make sense.

When you understand the concept of grace, you discover that you have permission to rest. You can get off the treadmill. You don't have to be working all the time to keep up your image or to achieve what somebody else has done. You can breathe, you can relax, you can enjoy being the person God created you to be.

Discovering rest as you experience a genuine, true concept of God is not a license to be lazy or to live as you please, nor does it give you a "get-out-of-jail-free card" or the freedom to do anything you want. Just the opposite. You have freedom to rest in the security of your Heavenly

Father's love. Then even our work is from an overflow of the joy and approval we've already received from God. That changes everything!

How?

For one thing, you realize that you no longer need to struggle and strive for His acceptance. The good news of the gospel of Jesus Christ is that God accepts you just as you are. You are welcome at His table. Does He approve of the evil things we say and do? Of course not. But when you stumble and fall, He is right there to pick you up and get you moving in the right direction again. He accepts *you* for who you are without the need to prove yourself worthy to be in His presence.

Jesus wants you to know that you matter, that you are worthy because of the forgiveness He offers; if you trust in Him, you are clean. Your past sins, failures, and mistakes are gone.

In Revelation 3, Jesus wrote a letter to the church at Laodicea from heaven. The Laodiceans had gotten so caught up in their prideful traditions that they had become passive about God. As Jesus called them back to relationship, He did so in the context of a meal: "See! I stand at the door and knock. If anyone hears my voice and opens the door, I will come in to him and eat with him, and he with me."[48]

Did you get that? Jesus wants to have meaningful mealtimes with *you*! And He will as you open up the door of your heart and trust Him, not only for your salvation and heaven in your future but for fellowship with you—to eat with you, to converse with you, to guide you every day of your life.

When you try to find fulfillment in anything or anybody else, you will be frustrated and unfulfilled, but if you trust Him, you can relax and know that He has you in His care. He has you in His hands, and He is able to take care of you. Stop striving; you can stop seeking acceptance or approval from other human beings because your heavenly Father says, "You are okay in My book. You are accepted; you are forgiven; you are clean. You are welcome at My table."

Moreover, consider this: it's only when you feel accepted at God's table that you are able to welcome others to yours in a safe way—in a way that they feel accepted too—whether your own family or friends. Ask yourself some probing questions: Do your kids feel accepted at your table? Or, do they think they're welcome only if they make the A, lead the team, get into the college? Are they hesitant to approach your table because they feel they haven't earned their place there?

Guess what? Because your heavenly Father says, "You are okay in My book. You are accepted," you have the freedom to accept your family members and friends, regardless of their performances. Now, there is a message our world desperately needs to know.

CHAPTER 8

The Blessing of the Table

On the Friday evening before my first Sunday morning at Kingsland, the church hosted a "meet and greet" in the church foyer so members of the congregation could welcome Lana and me prior to Sunday morning worship services. About six hundred people showed up, and Lana and I spoke with every one of them. By the time we were done, Lana was exhausted.

Several people going through the reception line said something such as, "There are a number of other people who wanted to be here but who couldn't come because they have another event to attend across the church campus."

"Really? What's going on?" I asked.

"Oh, we have a tradition here that before Graduation Sunday, we have a special banquet for our graduating seniors with their families," someone told me. "The parents share a meal with their families and write a blessing for their graduate, and they share it with their son or daughter that night."

"Oh, really?" I was intrigued. "Do you think it would be okay if Lana and I joined them?"

"Sure, that would be fine, but the event will be over soon."

As soon as we could, Lana and I eased away from the foyer and hurried across campus, slipping in to the banquet unobtrusively. This was where the real action was taking place. Around the tables, many of the people were wiping tears from their eyes as the dads and moms spoke words of blessing over their sons or daughters. No doubt, some of the parents had never before done something like that, saying things such as, "Bobby, this is what you mean to me; you are God's gift to your mother and me," or, "Christina, your thoughtfulness is a blessing to our family," or other words of blessing over their children.

The words being spoken in that room and around those tables were more powerful than most sermons, speeches, or songs I had ever heard. Parents and graduates alike left that night with smiles on their faces, a fresh appreciation for each other, and a new lilt in their steps as they faced the future.

One set of parents shared a blessing with their daughter that we now use as an example for other moms and dads of graduating seniors. Imagine the following letter being read aloud after dinner across a candlelit table from two loving parents to their daughter:

Jade,

Your mother and I want to tell you that we are very proud to have you in our family. God gave you to us, and we love you only second to God. You are a miracle and a gift that was made in His image. You have brought pure joy to our lives since the day you were born. We want you to know that we graciously affirm you in our family. You have a servant heart that will forever be remembered within our family, within all the churches you've served in, and within the many friends you've made during your journey. Your youth has been filled with many memories that will never be forgotten. To mention a few: . . .

Jade, we want to speak some wisdom into you and let you know how much we love you. Your mother and I have been praying for you and your husband since your childhood. We pray that you will give your future husband the single most important element of marriage, your purity. We pray you never sacrifice your purity for anyone outside of marriage. We also pray you will learn to love your husband like Jesus loves the church.

Jade, we also want you to know that you don't have to partake in any of the worldly sins to prove yourself to anyone. We encourage you to live for God and do what Jesus would do. You will never be perfect, but we desire you to have the courage to be the best you can be. The truth is, God empowers you with the Holy Spirit. Remember to use your strengths and abilities that God gave you to be a blessing to others. You have a new mission field to reach others for Christ. This is the Great Commission that we are called to participate in. God doesn't call the qualified. God qualifies the called.

Jade, you are entering into a part of life where you have to make decisions without the consultation of your father and mother. The one thing we want you to remember is that every decision has a consequence. We encourage you to be patient, pray, and don't think you have to make a decision without first asking God for His guidance. God loves you more than your father and mother. God will never leave you and He will always answer your prayers in His timing. Don't be afraid to wait. Our encouragement to you for the next four or five years is to continue working out, getting faster and stronger being the best soccer player you can be. At the same time, you have to make the best grades you can make. Be sure to maintain a healthy lifestyle. God wants you to be the best you can be, and you can't achieve that without being fit, lean, and fast. The Bible tells us that if we *compete we should always compete to win so when people look at us as winners we can give God the glory for all He's blessed us with. Always stay fit for God, your future husband, and your family so you can give your best at all times.*

Jade, drugs and alcohol are a part of life. You will be exposed to them more in college than you have ever experienced in your whole life. Our encouragement is to follow Jesus as an example. Never do drugs or get drunk and lose your witness. God has blessed you with special gifts and talents to bless others. Be the salt and light to others on your team and around campus. God will protect you. He is your refuge and will guide you in your ways.

Jade, you have made your father and mother so proud. We can see you in your future as a wonderful, loving wife and mother who is focused on teaching her children the Word of God. You would be an excellent stay-at-home mother, missionary, coach, teacher, or staff member of a church. You are an awesome teacher of the Bible. You have a loving heart for God and you live your life like Jesus; don't change. We want you to know that love isn't defined by money or anything monetary. Love is defined by your willingness to make God number one in your life, your husband number two in your life, and your children number three in your life. Love is defined in the Bible as discipline. Make sure your children are disciplined, know the Bible, and respect others.

Jade, your mother and I want to give you this letter of blessing with a promise that we will never stop loving and praying for you. You have been a joy to raise. You have blessed us, and we thank God for you every day. Good luck to you and your future. Never take your gaze off the cross, and always talk to God. We love you more than you'll ever know. Now go and make disciples of all nations, baptizing them in the name of the Lord Jesus Christ.

Love, Dad and Mom

Do the words spoken around the table really matter that much? More than you can imagine.

The words spoken around the table have enormous, significant weight. So why not use the time during meaningful mealtimes as opportunities to bless your family members? Certainly, blessing your family goes beyond the table, but it cannot be absent from the table.

What Does It Mean to Bless?

Nowadays, we can't take for granted that most people know what it means to bless someone. In many situations when the term *bless* is expressed in our culture, it is not being used in an accurate biblical sense.

If you sneeze in public, you may hear someone say, "God bless you," an age-old practice of unknown origin. One legend captured by William Butler Yeats in 1898 indicates people believed that sneezing was the body's natural attempt to ward off an invading evil spirit.[49] However the custom came about, it is remarkable how universal this practice is, and I don't think I've ever seen someone get offended by the response.

If you feel sorry for someone and are expressing compassion or sympathy, you may say, "Bless your heart." Of course, in many areas of the United States, that phrase is not always considered a kind expression. Depending on the circumstances, it may actually be a snide or sarcastic or otherwise uncomplimentary statement that might be more accurately translated, "Bless your heart, you are so stupid!"

At ball games or patriotic events, we often hear people singing, "God Bless America," but in most cases, they are not really singing a prayer to God. If the participants are thinking at all about the words they are singing, they are simply hoping that our nation will be safe and prosper. Certainly, safety and prosperity could be blessings, if appreciated and used properly, but there is much more to the matter.

So how does the Bible use the term *bless*, and why is it an important and valuable habit for us to establish the practice of blessing in our family?

In the Old Testament, the Hebrew word for *bless* literally means "to bow the knee." It is a term used to describe the giving of honor to another person. Another use of the word includes the idea of adding value, as if you were placing gold coins on a scale to demonstrate that something is worth far more than previously thought or understood. So when we bless another person, we are ascribing value to that person.

The word in the New Testament most often translated as *bless* literally means "a present given as a sign of gracious kindness." So if you put all these descriptions together, a simple way to define the practice of blessing another person is, "A blessing means to give honor by intentionally ascribing God's promises to another person."

Notice that this definition demands intentionality. It doesn't happen by accident or automatically. As an act of your will, you must *choose* to bless someone. But if that seems difficult, notice, too, the source of the blessing. It comes from God and the promises He has made, so it is not simply you lathering a child or spouse with a lavish but empty compliment. When you bless a person biblically and properly, your words have the full backing of God's promises. That's what makes your blessing so powerful!

To ascribe God's promises to another person means that you are assigning those promises from a source— God—to another person, perhaps your child, your spouse, friends, coworkers, or even your boss. So although you are not responsible to fulfill God's promises, you have the privilege of directing those promises to another person. That is important, because what you are really doing is not merely wishfully thinking, thinking happy thoughts, or bandying about grandiose words that have no backing. You are sharing what God has already said, so you can have confidence that His Word will be effective.

Now, you may be wondering, "If God has already said something, why do I need to reiterate it?"

Think of it this way. Imagine a couple that has inherited billions of dollars. They want for absolutely nothing. But on their anniversary, the husband goes out and buys his wife a beautiful diamond necklace. Why would he do that? She already has several gorgeous necklaces, and her name is on all the bank accounts so she has total access to their billions. After all, it is her money too. If she spots a necklace at the jewelry store, she could buy it for herself at any time.

So why does the husband think she will enjoy it?

Because his gift to her reminds her of what she has already been given, and it honors her as his wife.

In a similar manner, the Bible makes it clear that the blessings we offer to our kids or to our spouse or others aren't merely empty words. The blessing actually possesses the power to help move that person toward the fulfillment of the promise.

The Scripture says, "Therefore, be imitators of God, as dearly loved children, and walk in love, as Christ also loved us and gave himself for us, a sacrificial and fragrant offering to God."[50] This is more than simply lovey-dovey feelings or empty words. This is the standard that God has given, showing us how He wants us to love one another.

From that, we can draw two important insights. First, *you and I need a blessing.* No one is so independent and self-assured that he or she can survive without the blessing that God has in mind for that person. You were made to be blessed, and until you experience that affirmation, there will be a void in your life. You may not recognize that something is missing; you may not have a clue that you can or should be blessed, but without it, something will be missing in your life.

If you say, "Aww, I don't need a blessing. I'm doing just fine the way I am," let me clue you in on a little-known secret: even Jesus needed and received a blessing from His Father.

Have you ever noticed how His ministry began? He was baptized by John the Baptist, and then immediately He was blessed by His heavenly Father. Matthew 3:17 informs us, "And behold, a voice from heaven said, "This is my beloved Son, with whom I am well pleased" (ESV).

With these words, God was blessing His Son. And guess what? If Jesus needed and received a blessing, how much more do you and I?

When people miss out on the blessing, it's not like missing something that they never knew about anyhow. No, the absence of the blessing in your life leaves an awful void. One of the saddest passages in the Bible describes Esau, Isaac's firstborn son, crying out to his father for his blessing. In Old Testament times, two blessings were usually given, one to the firstborn son and then lesser blessings to the siblings. But in this case, unfortunately, Isaac had already conferred the firstborn's blessing on Esau's brother, Jacob, through a ploy spawned and abetted by Isaac's wife, Rebekah. Esau's plaintive cry preceded the poignant plea of millions of sons down through history. "When Esau heard his father's words, he cried out with a loud and bitter cry and said to his father, 'Bless me too, my father!'"[51]

I've heard similar words from all sorts of men and women and witnessed the crippling effects in their lives when they have been deprived of their father's blessing. The lack of blessing inevitably results in insecure men trying to cope with their pain and equally insecure women who desperately seek approval, often in unhealthy ways.

Truth is, we all long for a blessing. I was at a pastor's retreat some time ago and was sharing in a prayer time with a group of men, all of whom I greatly respected.

One of the pastors paused in our prayer time and pleaded with us, "I just want someone . . ." his normally strong voice quivered a bit as he completed his request, "to bless me." I witnessed five pastors surround him with a blessing, and it was beautiful . . . and powerful . . . and transformational in that man's life.

The second insight we can draw from Paul's words to the Ephesians is that *you and I were created to bless others.* Remember? Paul encourages us to be imitators of God, and what did God do?

Scripture says, "So God created man in his own image; he created him in the image of God; he created them male and female."[52] That means we have been created to reflect the nature of our Creator. Then immediately after He created Adam and Eve in the garden of Eden, God blessed them! So we have the privilege of reflecting God's image to one another by blessing one another.

When you imitate God, you will automatically love people the way He loves them, and that includes blessing them. Imagine that. You have been given an incredible power to positively change lives, just as God has changed yours. You can do that by offering your children, your spouse, and others a spoken or written blessing. And one of the best places to do that is around the dining table during your mealtimes together. The table presents a glorious opportunity for blessings for a number of reasons: Many of life's distractions are set aside as you sit across from one another face-to-face. Conversations that might otherwise feel awkward or contrived happen more naturally with the added comfort the food brings. Also, consistent rituals are easily built into the natural progression of the meal, such as going around the table to share the events of the day. Such rituals present wonderful opportunities to speak blessings over one another as you recount victories or put defeats into perspective.

But it doesn't stop there. When you invite others to the table with you—even those outside of your own household—God gives you the opportunity to speak words of blessing into the lives of people that He leads you to encourage or otherwise influence.

To be clear, a blessing is not the same as flattery. You are not celebrating something that hasn't already been established or accomplished. If your son is lazy, won't work, and is sponging off you and your spouse, you will not be blessing him by telling him, "Oh, son, you are such a hard worker. I'm so proud of you." No, that is not a blessing.

A blessing is speaking real promises that God has already made into the life of someone, regardless of how far he or she might be living from those promises at the moment you speak them. So if your son is a lazy, complacent sponge, rather than offering false compliments, tell him the truth as God sees him. "Son, I believe in you. God has uniquely gifted you for service. In fact, the Bible says that He is doing a work in your life right now and He will never leave you. I can imagine a wonderful future for you as you choose to obey the Lord and follow His commands. I love you, son, and I bless you."

What are you doing? You are not making up kind compliments out of thin air. No, you are saying the same things over your son that God has already declared about him.

How Can You Bless Someone?

How can you go about blessing your children or others in your life? John Trent believes there are five essential elements involved in an effective blessing:

- Meaningful touch
- A spoken (or written) message
- Attaching high value to the one being blessed
- Picturing a special future for the one being blessed
- An active commitment to fulfill the blessing[53]

In biblical times, a father wishing to bless his son might lay his hands on the son's shoulder or head, or he might hug and kiss the son, and his touch would communicate affirmation. This sort of spiritual touch often communicated the transfer of power, healing, financial blessing, or authority. The practice of the "laying on of hands" carried over to New Testament believers when they prayed for individuals and anointed them for ministry and other service. It is still common today in many congregations when a new pastor is installed.

Speaking words of blessing may seem like an obvious step, but it's critical that those words are intentional and verbally given. Why would anyone neglect to actually *say* the words of blessing? First of all, it is an emotionally vulnerable act. For many people, they've never received or exchanged such statements, and it can feel overwhelming to actually state them. Regardless of how challenging such a step may seem, it's absolutely worth it. Yes, I've heard stories of blessings that were given but not well received by hard-hearted people, so there is a real risk in some cases for opening your heart in this way. But I've never heard of someone who in the long run regretted saying the words of blessing they had for the ones they loved. In fact, if such words seem awkward in your family's historic norms, one way to make them less awkward is to say them over a meal. After praying for your food, and as others are passing plates, you have the perfect opportunity to say, "I hope we never take for granted what a gift it is to be together when we can. In fact, I've been reminded lately, _____, of how honored I am to be your father/mother/spouse/son/daughter/friend. I want you to know what you mean to me."

Speaking those words of blessing aloud is important. Something amazing often happens as the words move from the hearer's ears, to the mind, to the subconscious, all the way to the heart. It is not enough to believe them or to think them in your mind. Say the words aloud to the person you want to bless.

Words have enormous power to build up and encourage a person, or words can tear a person to pieces. If you are a parent, your kids need to hear words of blessing from you. Husbands and wives need positive words of affirmation as well. You can't assume that someone understands your good intentions or high hopes; you must put the blessing into words. Even if you write out a blessing, it still possesses more power to the recipient if you read the words aloud. Something connects in a special way in the heart and mind of a person when he or she hears those words of blessing spoken aloud.

In the actual words of your blessing, use terms to convey high value that is consistent with what God says about the person. Emphasize the person's qualities that align with biblical traits, such as courage, honesty, or the fruit of the Holy Spirit: love, joy, peace, patience, kindness, goodness, faithfulness, gentleness, and self-control. You can't go wrong blessing someone with those spiritual attributes that God wants all of us to have. Keep in mind, you are trying to express that this person is highly valued by God and by you.

Part of what makes a blessing effective are words that describe a picture of how this blessing is going to show up in the person's future. You don't need to possess a special gift of prophecy to do that; simply present the picture of hope that God has given to you to impart to the person you are blessing.

The final element of the blessing is an active commitment on your part to help see that blessing come to pass in the life of the person you are blessing. This is about making sure the one you are blessing knows this isn't a momentary decision but rather a firm conviction in their core identity. It means that you will actively support the person and pray that God's plans for him or her will come to pass. Of course, part of that commitment is the decision to regularly sit down to meals together to share life, catch up, and make the blessing last.

The reclaiming of your table's legacy involves looking back into the past; in many ways, even the redeeming of your table's legacy is God's restoration and buying back of that which was lost around your table. But the blessing of the table is looking to the future, blessing your children or your spouse, ascribing God's promises to them so they can enjoy all that God has for them not merely in the present but in the days and years ahead as well. The words shared over food, eating with your family, have tremendous weight and power in the lives of your family members.

How Does That Start with the Kids?

If you want to ascribe God's promises to your kids, you will need to study your children so you can confirm their strengths. The blessing will be meaningless if it does not apply now or potentially in the future. Of course, since our kids are all different, you may not want to use the same blessing for each one. Instead, personalize your words so each child knows that the words you are ascribing to him or her are meant personally.

When Grandma Rush (Dad's mom) passed away several years ago, our girls were still around elementary school age. There were plenty of heirs to receive Grandma's few possessions, so I wasn't expecting anything. I was grateful, however, to receive one unique plate that had been in her kitchen for years. You might have heard of or seen a "You Are Special Today" plate, a concept that originated with the German company Waechtersbach in 1832. The idea is to pull out this bright red plate on special occasions to highlight one member of the family and celebrate him or her during the mealtime. It was a simple way to turn birthdays, good report cards, or anniversaries of spiritual milestones into moments where mealtimes became vehicles for memorable, intentional blessings. Those plates are readily available today, but you can use almost any unique object to elevate the moment, turning a mealtime into the opportunity for a blessing.

At Kingsland, blessing one another is the number one habit that we want to see in our homes. Why? Because homes that bless thrive. Where there is no blessing, it doesn't matter what else you do; everything else becomes simply a performance.

On the other hand, where the dad is blessing the children, mom and dad are blessing each other, and the kids are blessing the parents, there is a power in that family that is nearly impossible to overcome.

I've been serving families in church ministry for three decades, and I don't think it's an exaggeration to say we're surrounded every day by people who feel disconnected from their loved ones and long for the blessing of those closest to them. But it doesn't have to be this way. As James Taylor famously sang, "Much better to shower the people you love with love," and the most transformational way to give that love is by ascribing God's promises to one another. And one of the easiest places to do this is around the family table as you enjoy five meaningful mealtimes together each week.

CHAPTER 9

The Shared Table

While speaking at Kingsland on the subject of the open table, my friend Randy Phillips displayed a popular T-shirt he had recently seen for sale. The shirt read, "LOVE THY NEIGHBOR." Then beneath the familiar slogan were these words:

Thy Homeless Neighbor
Thy Muslim Neighbor
Thy Black Neighbor
Thy Gay Neighbor
Thy White Neighbor
Thy Jewish Neighbor
Thy Christian Neighbor
Thy Atheist Neighbor
Thy Racist Neighbor
Thy Addicted Neighbor

With the T-shirt displayed on the large screen in the sanctuary, Randy then facetiously voiced what many people may have been thinking. "That's just too much diversity for me," Randy said. "I can't do that. That just pushes me out of my comfort zone."

He pointed at the picture of the T-shirt on the screen. "I am not comfortable with that," he said with a twinkle in his eye. "I would rather close ranks, [and] stay with the people I'm comfortable with. That causes too much tension for me."

Randy continued, "This is not ideal but this is real . . . these are the people that I live and work with . . . these are the people that God has strategically placed in my path. What do I do about that list?"

Randy answered his own question: "I have to set another place at the table for them."

What would we even talk about? you're wondering.

That's the great adventure. You meet people who may be different from you and you look beyond the faults to see the need. No, you don't have to compromise your convictions. But when share your table with them and ask, "Please tell me your story," you earn the right to speak the truth in love. Trust is earned through relationship, and relationships are often built across the table.

Go Sit at Someone's Table and Change the World

When Lana was trying to find her place at Kingsland, someplace where she could serve in a way that held meaning and significance to her, she didn't jump into teaching a class at church or helping in the nursery. Instead, she waited, prayed for wisdom, and soon found her own passionate ministry. But it was far outside the usual Kingsland parameters.

A mere ten-to-fifteen-minute drive away from affluent Katy is a section of town known as Brookshire. It is less than a dozen miles away out in the country, yet it is an entirely different world from the one in which most of our parishioners live.

An impoverished area where Civil War–era slaves once gathered after the Emancipation Proclamation, Brookshire feels like an inner-city community, even though it is not. It has all the usual negative elements that breed despair: unemployment, drug addiction, crime, absentee fathers, and hopelessness. Kingsland "adopted" it and built a community center in Brookshire. We dubbed the center The Hangar.

Originally, Lana wanted to do an after-school tutoring program there and then feed the kids dinner. But before long she found a group of adult women, most of whom were low-come, minority women, African American or

Hispanic. Many of them were married to husbands who are in prison; some of the women themselves had been incarcerated previously. A number of the women struggled with alcohol or drug addictions, and several were former prostitutes.

Lana and a few of her friends initiated friendly get-togethers with some of the women in Brookshire. "We're not going there to teach or sing or do churchy kinds of things," Lana instructed her friends. "We're not going to have Bible studies or read a book. We're just going out to have a simple dinner and talk around the table, to build relationships with the women and be their friends."

We were already working with some of the teenagers in the area, but there was nothing for the moms. Lana explained her motivation to several of her friends: "I want to work with the women of Brookshire. They have no sense of normal. Many of them have husbands who are in prison. They live in fear."

"But what can we do?" one of Lana's friends asked. "Their needs are overwhelming. Where can we start?"

Lana said, "I'm going to go cook for these women every Monday."

Lana began meeting regularly with a few women in March 2018 simply by inviting them to gather for a free dinner and conversation. Around the table, the group talked about issues that mattered to the women. Lana encouraged the women to invite their friends—and they did. To make it easier for the Brookshire women to attend, Lana encouraged them to bring their children along with them to dinner each week. Many of the women were glad to bring their kids because they couldn't afford babysitters. Since most of the Brookshire kids had never been in Sunday school classes or other kinds of church environments, they were sometimes more rowdy or noisy than other children. But they responded well to love.

Before long, Lana was fixing dinner every Monday evening for thirty ladies and their children. They ate together and talked. That was it. No program, no agenda, just food and conversation. In the beginning, Lana made all the food, but donors soon came on board to help.

Lana named the group *Gather* because that was their main purpose. As she suggested, they had no formal program. Occasionally, a friend might go with Lana to share her testimony with the Brookshire women, but mostly the Gather group was simply about food and friendship around the table. Their sole purpose in getting together was to share a meal and tell their stories to each other. The women grew increasingly more committed and excited about being there.

The meals were usually something simple such as beef stew or chicken pot pie. In a most fitting corollary, one of the favorite meals among the Brookshire women became Lorie Pendergrass's family chicken pot pie recipe with cranberry sauce. Lorie gave the recipe to Lana, and now, at least once a month, Lana has chicken pot pie with the women in Brookshire using Lorie's family recipe.

Lana continued that routine for more than two years, and it eventually spun off several other groups that are gathering in Brookshire. The walls are down and dozens of ladies are able to interact openly and honestly. God has restored and redeemed the table in Brookshire; it is a table of blessing, and it is now a shared table. In the process, the women have grown to trust one another, and slowly but surely, they have opened up to one another and real spiritual commitments have happened, almost as an "accidental" result.

For Lana, the value of the Brookshire ministry has nothing to do with being the pastor's wife. It is about compassion for people who are struggling and need to know that there is a God who cares about their needs. People who don't find some way to give of themselves eventually dry up—usually sooner rather than later. But as the Scripture says, "Whoever brings blessing will be enriched, and one who waters will himself be watered."[54] Those who keep going and keep giving of themselves are revived and refreshed.

The Turquoise Table

If you will look outward by going to someone else's table or inviting others to yours, you may be surprised at the positive influence and significance you might discover. Sharing a table together lowers walls, builds understanding, and helps people to find common ground. So be creative in searching for ways to share a table with others.

Sometimes loving your neighbor means loving the person who literally lives next door. But it can also mean finding a way to share a table with people who might otherwise pass you by.

Kristin Schell has found a practical way to live this out in Austin, Texas, where she lives. She purchased a picnic table, painted it turquoise, and rather than putting it on her back patio, she placed the picnic table in the front yard, where people passing by the house could see it. Each day, she placed a basket of flowers and some cookies and lemonade or water on the table for anyone who wanted some free refreshments.

None did. For a while, joggers passed by and simply looked at her as though she had lost her mind. Others walking by ignored her completely.

But Kristin continued her routine, placing goodies on the table each day for anyone who wanted to take them or for anyone who wished to sit down and rest while waiting for their kids' school bus to arrive. Before long, some neighbors took her up on her offer.

It was while sitting around the picnic table with people in the neighborhood that Kristen learned that the woman living next door had breast cancer. The couple across the street was getting a divorce, and the married couple down the street hadn't heard from their son in more than two years. People began to open their hearts to Kristin as they shared time around the table. No, she didn't have all the answers to their problems. But she knew the One who did, and real transformations took place in that neighborhood because one woman dared to invite some people to share her table. She's now shared this vision to thousands through her book, *The Turquoise Table*.

Often, when you share the table, you find yourself in a position to help redeem somebody else's table. Nobody should have to eat alone. Instead, make some extra food and leave a chair open at your table for someone else to join you—especially people who are different from you, who may not look, think, or vote like you. Or maybe they don't root for the same teams you do or hang out with your Christian friends. They may not even believe in God. Or perhaps there is someone you know who could never repay you for what you do for him or her. Make room for that person around your table.

Shared Table, Shared Value

What's the difference between a transaction and a relationship? Sometimes the difference is simply a shared meal. My mind goes back to the account of Zaccheaus in Luke 19. Zacchaeus, a chief tax collector by trade, was perhaps the most despised man in Jericho. When he had the opportunity, however, he tried to get to Jesus. There was perhaps no one less worthy of time with the Son of God, and yet we read about Jesus sharing a meal, Zacchaeus coming to faith, and a life transformed. What a story he had to tell for the rest of his life: "I was about as far from God as possible. But Jesus ate with me of all people, and I was never the same!"

Elevating the value of a person doesn't always require connections with those who are philosophically different than you. Sometimes the difference is cultural, economic, or even geographic. The first time our daughter, Ryley, and I went to Guatemala on a mission trip, we went with our group to a trash dump outside of town, where the people were scavenging for food in the garbage. The missions group did what most American missions groups do: we set up a portable pavilion where we could feed dinner to the impoverished, hungry people. The way in which we addressed the hunger issues, however, demonstrated how disconnected even compassionate acts can come across without the power of the shared table.

While I'm certain our in-country partners who arranged the feeding centers had their reasons, the scene came across as a typical top-down way to do humanitarian work, reinforcing the misconceptions that many people in third world countries believe about "ugly

Americans." The volunteers got off the bus carrying large vats of soup, and there were scores of kids with no shoes who didn't speak English, lined up along with their moms (and occasionally their dads) for more than a hundred yards, waiting to receive their allotment of soup in the small bowls provided by the missions group.

With the best of intentions, the volunteers greeted each person: "Hi, how are you? So good to see you!" The volunteers filled the person's bowl, handed it back to him or her, and said, "Have a nice day. Jesus loves you."

There were two significant breakdowns in the plan as I saw it: First, we were feeding the people for the day but doing nothing to change their long-term circumstances. Instead, I felt as though we were saying by our actions, "You are poor and unable, and are not worthy, so we're bringing you a meal for the day, and maybe some food that will last a few weeks." Second, there was no relationship being cultivated between us and these precious people, or even between themselves through the joy of shared meals.

When Ryley and I got back to our cabin that evening, we agreed, "We need to do more. What if we were to adopt a village and work here on a long-term basis?"

Out of that experience, the Austin-Guatemala Project was born. I'm indebted to my friend Chris King who stepped up to pilot this long-term project for several years to coordinate the many churches and people who accepted the challenge to make our food distribution efforts more meaningful. On our return trips, we still brought food, but we also shared the table with hundreds of locals. In addition to the food, we brought skilled people to teach sewing and other crafting skills. We established a system of "micro loans" so the local people could establish their own businesses by purchasing supplies such as ovens for baking or greenhouses for vegetables and farming. Then, we sold some of their products in the United States. We learned the names of people in the community and knew some of their kids' names as well. We worked side by side with our new friends to build a school for the children and homes for the poor, and we planted a church for the spiritually hungry.

In the midst of these many journeys and extensive developments, delicious food was always a common denominator. Given the resources they needed, the wonderful people of Pueblo Modelo had no problem preparing mouthwatering meals! And every time good things happened, food was not far behind: whether it was the money that came in from sales of purses in the United States, food from the many new gardens, or meat from the new chickens, food brought life to the village.

We also planted fruit trees along the road. The fruit trees provided shade, streets without dust, and perhaps most importantly, produce. There was life and sustenance where there used to be scarcity. All sorts of good things followed the food. Everything changed when the food came, and even better, transformation took place when that food was shared.

We went back to Guatemala numerous times, and Lana and I fell in love with the food there, tasty but not spicy. Much of the food we ate during our subsequent stays was cooked by a group of older women. They created some special meals consisting of meat, beans, vegetables, and sweet, fried plantains. Our meals together in Guatemala were never fancy, but my, were they ever special!

You may discover that the sharing of meaningful mealtimes around your table with a person who is not a family member or a close relative may produce some of the most meaningful moments, the best friendships, and deepest significance in your life. You may even want to get in the habit of leaving a special chair open at your table for a potential guest or as a reminder to seek out people who may benefit from being around the table with you and your family. One family with whom I am familiar likes to designate a chair around their table as "the Lord's chair," reminding them to invite Jesus to share every meal with them.

You can invite somebody to your table or you can go to their table, even if you have a table of your own. If someone asks you to share their table, say yes if you can. Consider it an honor and an opportunity to build or strengthen that relationship.

CHAPTER 10

A Table That Fills in the Gaps

As believers in Jesus, we are called to help fill the gaps in families that have someone missing, whether it is an absentee dad, a single mom, a widow, or a senior citizen who needs help. The church is called to fill in the gaps in whatever way is possible. One of the easiest ways to do that is simply to invite someone to eat with you, especially someone who has no other family members in close proximity.

Regardless of what you experience in life, if you will allow God to redeem it, He can use even your negative hurt and pain and turn your past experiences into a positive blessing in your life and the lives of others—if you will allow Him.

An only child of two parents who tried for many years to conceive, Hope was often told that she was a "prayer baby," an answer to prayer. Unfortunately, her dad didn't see it that way for long. Hope recalls, "When I was only three years of age, Dad left; Mom had to explain that Dad was gone and not coming back home.

"When I was nine years old, we moved to Texas to be closer to Dad, but I constantly struggled with a sense of rejection. I decided to love him and honor him, but I kept my expectations low. I had a hard time handling the truth that I was not a priority to my father."

As a single parent, Hope's mom raised her well. She had a supportive church family and sacrificed to keep her daughter in a Christian school. But that safe environment turned out not so safe for Hope.

"I was sexually mistreated as a child by a custodian in the school," Hope recalls. "Later, as a young teenager, I was again taken advantage of by a neighbor. I never told my mom about the sexual abuse, but the Lord rescued me from that situation.

"It wasn't until years later, after I was married, that I sought counseling to help me deal with the emotional pain I still carried from those experiences. In trauma therapy sessions, I was able to write out my forgiveness of the people who had hurt me, and I asked the Lord for emotional healing regarding those events in my childhood. It was only then that those negative experiences lost their power over me.

"Still, I lived with a heightened wariness of all men," Hope recalls.

Hope's world was rocked again at age fourteen when her mom was diagnosed with breast cancer and had to take early retirement. She battled the cancer for more than eleven years before succumbing to it, when Hope had barely turned twenty-five years old.

Despite knowing that her mom was with the Lord in heaven, Hope's life spiraled downward beginning the evening of her mom's memorial service.

Hope says, "That night, at twenty-five years of age, I allowed myself to be in a morally compromising situation, and I gave up my virginity. It was an isolated event, but my moral lapse resulted in me getting pregnant. I learned the hard way that anyone can fall.

"We decided to get married only because I was pregnant. We didn't consider other compatibility factors. He claimed to be a believer, and I was grateful for the compassion he expressed for me following Mom's passing, so within five months of me finding out that I was pregnant, we married."

"Our daughter, Emma, was born in April 1999. She gave my husband and me a common bond and a mutual purpose. We loved her completely. We found a strong church community, but my husband and I did not seek out the wise Christian counsel we needed to help us cope as a married couple, much less as parents.

"No matter how hard I tried, I could never capture my husband's sole attention. I was still operating out of the wilderness of wanting a man to love me, but I had no idea how that was to work. I had no real model for what a Christian marriage should look like.

"In July 2001, the Lord blessed us with another beautiful daughter, Abby. My husband and I both loved being parents. But there seemed to be walls that we couldn't get over, and strongholds in my husband's life that we couldn't address. So I focused on raising our girls to love and walk with Jesus, while waiting for the Lord to heal and restore our marriage.

"Only four years after our wedding, the Lord revealed ongoing unfaithfulness in our marriage. I talked to several wise counselors, in particular to pastors that my husband respected. One pastor offered to hold our hands and walk us through the restoration process.

"My husband was not willing, so with the sad blessing of the spiritual mentors, we divorced."

The rejection was devastating for Hope. "I remember going to bed and saying, 'Lord, it's okay if You don't wake me up. This hurts too bad and I don't think I can do this.'"

Hope had seen her own mother walk through the single-parenting experience, but nothing had touched her as deeply as the failure of her own marriage. Yet she never complained.

"If the Lord restores my marriage, I need to be healthy," she said. She spent long hours studying the

Word of God, exploring what it meant to recover from divorce, and how to have a healthy marriage. She led a Bible study and earned the respect of the women. Holding the Bible to her heart, Hope told the women, "Ladies, when this is all you have, you'll discover that this is all you need."

All the while, she home-schooled her daughters. Hope committed herself to being the primary faith trainer in her family. Her marriage was not restored, but for sixteen years, she poured into the life of her daughters and other women. She kept the girls involved in church and worked hard to instill Godly principles in her daughters, and the girls loved the people of Kingsland who also poured into their lives. The girls were able to spend time with Kingsland families that had the family structure that Hope and her daughters did not have. They were able to see strong Christian families modeled in front of them.

Occasionally, one of the girls came home bawling because they didn't have that same family structure, and Hope would have to reassure her daughters that God was her "husband" and He would also be the girls' Father. For the most part, though, the people of Kingsland filled in the gaps in Hope's family life and the girls knew they were loved and safe.

Occasionally, Hope asked a few of her married female friends to check with their husbands on certain issues so she could avoid a distorted or myopic view of family life. She didn't keep her search for wisdom a secret. Instead, she informed the girls which adults that she was leaning on for advice. "They help me to decide things for you," she told her daughters.

Hope also invited Lana and me to be sounding boards and to give her some wisdom regarding the way she was guiding her daughters. The girls always seemed to appreciate getting our perspective.

Perhaps because of her own experiences and the impact of infidelity on her family, Hope is remarkably wise and careful about anything that might be questionable. For instance, to remain above reproach and to avoid even a hint of impropriety, she always includes Lana and me in the same text message, even though we've been friends for quite a while. That is not being overly sensitive or prudish. In the world in which we live, that is simply being smart.

Hope sent a note to us asking, "Would you and Lana be willing to meet with Abby and provide some insight? Abby has some questions and it might be good for her to hear answers from a Christian man's perspective." Hope spoke straightforwardly, "When I say some things to the girls, they just hear me being the overprotective mom, scared to death that my daughters might make some of the same mistakes that I did."

"Well, that's understandable," I said. "That's what you are. You're a mom who is worried that your daughters might do as you did. That's okay. None of us want our kids to make the same mistakes we did if we can possibly help them to avoid those hurtful things."

Lana and I met with Hope and Abby for crepes at a café near our home and gathered around the table for dessert. It wasn't a conscious decision to meet around the table, but because we met there, rather than in my office or even in Hope's home, the walls went down much more easily and we all felt more comfortable in conversing about some delicate matters.

At first, Abby stared at her food as Hope broached the awkward subject. "I'm concerned about the young man that Abby is dating, that he is trying to taking advantage of her," she said straightforwardly.

Between bites of delicious strawberry crepes smothered in whipped cream and sips of a Lavender latte, a first for me, I was able to say, "Abby, you are a young woman of immense worth. Your mom and dad love you, but do you know how much God loves you? How He adores you and how much value you have to Him? Don't ever devalue yourself." It was a message that I would share with our own daughters or with other young men and women in the church, but it seemed to be much more palatable over crepes, and Abby received it well.

Abby realized that we weren't attacking her, and she responded positively, realizing that she could change for the better and make better choices for her life.

Beyond that, Lana and I got to be a small part of Hope's healing as well because she had invited us to join her and her daughter around the table.

Hope explains, "I wanted my daughters to know that even though they were living in a single-parent situation, they could be the recipients of wisdom from a number of married moms and dads too."

Lana and I were impressed with Hope's straightforward honesty with her daughters. Hope refused to be a victim. She was not bashful about saying, "Girls, this is not the normal biblical model for a family, but here we are. Here's what we can do. First, we are going to look at what biblical manhood looks like, so you can better know what kind of husband to look for, and even more important, so you will understand the Father heart of God."

Hope also wanted her two beautiful daughters to see and understand submission to authority. The way she did that was having people in her life to whom she could turn to for Godly counsel. When a conflict came up at home, Hope told her kids, "These are some of the people that we are going to ask for advice." Her daughters understood that there were some blind spots in their mom's vision, but by depending on the insights of other godly parents, they could all benefit.

When it came to male role models for her daughters, Hope was stringent and protective about which men could be around the girls. "I am convinced, as the Scripture says, 'He who walks with the wise will be wise,' so I was not willing to allow just anybody to transmit their values to my daughters." I was particular about the fathers of their friends who could speak into their lives, but we were blessed that there were plenty of godly men in our community groups and in the church. Our pastors stayed close to us as well, and the girls grew up knowing that there were strong men and good examples in their lives."

In October 2018, Hope began working in our Freedom Ministry, and she has sat across the table from hundreds of women with similar stories since that time. In each instance, she's had the opportunity to share far more than a good meal. Hope's is a story of redemption and healing. She's now the proud mother of two strong, healthy, and beautiful young adult daughters who are thriving on their own and walking with the Lord. God has brought her full circle. Hope is not only an example of what happens when a single mom makes a commitment to the table; she's an example for many of our single mothers of how to invite others around that table who can help provide the support they need.

When I made the challenge to our congregation a few years ago to commit to five meaningful mealtimes a week with the ones they loved, I was certainly aware that this might be especially daunting for the single adults in our church. I tried to address the need in two ways: First, I asked our members who lived with other family members to be proactive in welcoming others who might live alone. Second, I encouraged singles to be intentional about seeking out others in our church family, single or otherwise, to join them at the table for regular meals. What happened for many wasn't just a "check the box" invitation to others for dinner, but genuine friendships were born and deepened as people discovered God's design for the church as an extended family.

TABLE STORY

Mike

When I was serving as a pastor in Austin, a young man named Mike began attending our church. He was in his late twenties and single, which was not the primary demographic in our suburban church. Mike had moved to Austin after having served two tours in the army and was working at Camp Mabry, a large National Guard base in the area. I got to know Mike, and we really hit it off. He was a bright, quiet guy who'd lived a lot of life for a young, single man. In between his two tours, he'd managed to obtain his bachelor's and master's degrees at the University of Alabama. While in the military, Mike had risen to the rank of captain.

I invited Mike out to share lunch with me, and one lunch turned into another. We spent a number of lunch hours at Rudy's Bar-B-Q, a popular chain in Austin, eating brisket and smoked turkey off butcher's paper and drinking iced tea out of plastic cups, with country music playing in the background.

I knew that Mike had a messed-up childhood, but I had no idea about some of the experiences that had shaped his life. "Mike, tell me your story," I asked.

He did, piece by agonizing piece.

As we got to know each other, our brief chats became more of a mentoring relationship. I learned that Mike's father was an alcoholic, had left the family when Mike was young, and was mostly out of his life. I also learned that as a child Mike had been sexually assaulted by his uncle and had suffered the trauma of his mother and grandmother telling him, "You just need to keep quiet about it. Ignore the incident and move on." He then endured the heartache of watching his mother die from cancer—all before his twenty-third birthday.

By God's grace, a few years prior, Mike had a chance meeting with a Christian family in an Alabama airport. The family invited him to share a meal with them. They "adopted" Mike as their own, and, sitting around their table, for the first time in his life, he found a group of people who cared about him without expecting anything in return.

That's how he found the church where I pastored. When he moved to Austin, he didn't want to find a "cool church" where his age group was attending. He wanted to attend a church that reminded him of the one place where he had experienced an environment resembling a family. That was us.

I certainly didn't take the place of that dear family, but I tried to be the next best thing during Mike's time in Austin. We'd get together for coffee or just sit for an hour or two in my office and talk about life. Mike knew he could call me any time of the day or night, and no question was off limits. Mike remained in the army reserve during his hybrid civilian/government contract position at Camp Mabry. One day, he shared with me that he had been asked to serve on one more three-month mission overseas.

"Where will you be stationed?" I asked.

"I'm not allowed to say," Mike replied.

With that answer, I understood the gravity of Mike's next deployment. We prayed together for wisdom, and Mike felt confident that he should return on this trip. It was an act of patriotism but also a financial bonus for a young, single man.

While Mike was serving on this mission, I sometimes received phone calls at strange hours of the evening from unlisted numbers. Mike would be on the other end of the line in some top-secret place—just wanting to talk about life.

When Mike returned from this "mini-tour," he made the decision to go to see his father—something he hadn't done in more than five years. His dad was living in the Pacific Northwest, and two things seemed clear: this man could not have cared less about Mike, yet Mike was desperate for a relationship with him.

Prior to his departure, I warned Mike about getting his hopes up, but I also admired his tenacity in seeking to share the gospel with his father. Four days later, at nearly midnight, I received a call from Mike on my cell phone. This soldier who'd served in some of the toughest war zones on earth was weeping uncontrollably. When he finally regained enough composure to talk, he told me about his visit with his father.

Their dinner had been cordial, but Mike's dad had obviously been drinking before he arrived and certainly wasn't slowing down because of the visit. Mike knew if he waited until his dad was sober there would be no conversation, so he just took the plunge: he told his dad he missed him, and would love to reconnect in some way with his father.

Instead of considering the thought, Mike's dad ridiculed the request, insinuating that he was disappointed that a grown man would still be so desperate for his daddy to love him. He declared that his son was a failure and that he wasn't interested in dredging up the past. Mike's dad said, "When are you ever going to grow up and stop being such a big baby? Why do you need my love so much?"

By that time, his dad was drunk, and said, "Why don't you just get out of my life?"

Mike walked out of the house into the chilly night to take a walk and think about his next move. And then he called me. "My dad rejected me outright," he told me.

I don't remember exactly what I said, but I know it was something along the lines of, "You have demonstrated incredible grace by going there, Mike. And now you can leave with no regrets. You can be sure everything he is saying is born out of his own wounds. It is not only untrue but completely false. Mike, that's not who you are," I said.

"You don't need your dad's approval to be fulfilled. You have your heavenly Father's approval and you certainly have mine. I love you, Mike. And I am so proud of you."

Mike has had minimal contact with his father since that encounter.

Not long after that, Mike moved to Washington, DC, and got a job with a high-level government agency. I've since toured DC with him, and he does have a cool though ambiguous badge. He's still single, has dated a few nice girls, but is still waiting for "the one." We talk a few times a year by phone, and he also traveled with me to Israel a couple of years ago.

I tell you that story not because of what it meant to Mike for me to become a "father to the fatherless," but because it led to one of *my* most meaningful moments on my journey as a pastor and family advocate.

Father's Day is a marvelous celebration, but it is a little different for a pastor. I've always felt loved on Father's Day, but it's a workday for me. Ordinarily, I'm preaching multiple times, after which my family and I may go out to eat, and then I get to take a nap that afternoon.

The Father's Day after Mike moved to DC, however, was one I'll never forget. Just about the time I got home from church, enjoyed a meal with my family, and got into my blue jeans, my phone rang. I saw that it was Mike. I was thrilled to hear from him, as it had been a while, so I picked up the phone. "Hey Mike! Have you met the girl of your dreams?"

"Not yet! But I haven't stopped looking!"

"What can I do for you?"

"Nothing at all. I just wanted to call and wish you a happy Father's Day. You know things haven't turned out so well with my dad. But God has placed you in my life, and He's given me some men like you to look up to. And I'm thankful."

I said, "Mike, do you understand your value to God?"

"Yes, sir, I think I do, now."

Mike has been to the table. He has another table now, a spiritual table.

I don't think that I became a father to Mike, as that was more the role of his "Alabama family." But it was overwhelming to me that when he thought of who had filled the void that his natural family had caused in him, he included me. In that phone call, I got to experience the incredible blessing of representing the Father-heart of God, the empowerment of our family, the body of Christ as a "family of families," and a father to the fatherless. Moreover, I witnessed a glimpse of a legacy that extended beyond my immediate family that could impact future generations—and it all began with Mike and me having a meal around a rustic table.

CHAPTER 11

The Table in the Storm

Hurricane Harvey, a Category 4 hurricane, made landfall in Texas and Louisiana on August 25, 2017, causing more than $125 billion in destruction.

At least sixty-eight people died as a direct result of Hurricane Harvey, with more than forty other deaths due to indirect causes such as electrocution, traffic accidents, or the inability to get vital medicines. Making matters worse, the hurricane stalled for several days, hovering over Louisiana and Texas, lashing the area with winds up to 130 miles per hour and dumping more than a trillion gallons of water on the area. The damages were mind-boggling. More than thirteen million people were affected, 135,000 homes were destroyed, and nearly a million cars were flooded or wrecked.[55]

Earlier in the month, J. P. and Jessie Pruett and their children took a special picture standing in front of their house. It was the one-year anniversary of the family moving into their new home.

The downpour that drenched Houston for three days was equivalent to the amount of rain the area normally received in a year. As the water began to rise in the Pruetts' neighborhood all the way to their doorstep, the family huddled together and prayed, "God, we know that You have the power to work a miracle to stop this water from coming into our house, or you can work a miracle in the way that You provide for us afterward. We trust You either way."

J. P. recalls, "Our next-door neighbors came to spend the night with us because their home was only a one-story structure. So we invited them to stay with us where they would be safe. But before long, we had three feet of water in our house too. We quickly moved everybody upstairs and spent the night there."

Meanwhile, Jessie's phone blew up with calls and texts from people trying to find a way to help. Kingsland's missions pastor, Omar Garcia, was working to send a boat to rescue them. The kids' rooms were upstairs, so they were able to salvage their clothes, but everything downstairs was inundated with three feet of muddy, brackish water.

Three young men from Kingsland, who had heard that the family was stranded, maneuvered a boat down through the neighborhood streets to rescue the Pruett family and their neighbors. The rescuers took the evacuees to the home of another family in the church, where they found refuge around another shared table.

It was nine days before J. P. and Jessie were permitted to return to their home. They were devastated to see the destruction the water had wreaked and a bit overwhelmed by the repair work that needed to be done. Like most people in their neighborhood, the Pruetts carried no flood insurance on their property.

Both J. P.'s and Jessie's automobiles were destroyed by flood, one in the garage and one in the driveway, but the Lord provided cars for them through others. Someone gave J. P. a car with three hundred thousand miles on it, but it still ran well. "It was an awesome car," J. P. recalls, "and I loved it! The boys called it 'Dad's Luxury SUV.'"

Following the flood caused by Hurricane Harvey, J. P. and Jessie turned a negative experience to a positive by spending extra time around the table, using some key devotions with their children about God's protection and His provision for their family.

Despite the devastation in their lives, they said, "Let's hang on to what we know to be true, and remind our kids how God has blessed us in the past." Many deeply meaningful conversations and prayers took place around the family's kitchen table. Both parents felt passionate about including the kids in how the Lord was at work in their family. Whether good or bad, they wanted to share this part of life with their children.

Before the hurricane, the family had a flat-screen television over the fireplace mantle in their living room. After Harvey, as they were getting the house back together, Jessie said, "Let's put something over the mantle that reminds us of the goodness of God. So we put a painted verse over the mantle, 'For the Lord is good; His love endures forever, and His faithfulness continues for all generations.' It is a constant reminder that no matter what we go through, God will be with us."

* * * * *

More than six thousand people in our Houston community lost their homes to the hurricane and flooding; more than one thousand families in Katy alone lost their homes; at least one hundred families in our immediate Kingsland circle lost their homes. Many more were temporarily forced out of their homes into makeshift shelters. Beyond helping our own church members to escape the floodwaters, it broke my heart to see so many people living on cots in the shelters. I knew we had to do something, and I believed that if we could rally our fellow Christians in Katy, we could be effective in helping our community. I hoped, too, that we could bring in the family ministry element as well as helping to meet basic physical needs.

Following the hurricane and the subsequent widespread flooding, we knew that the cleanup and rebuilding efforts would be massive. Rather than waiting on government assistance, three days after Harvey hit, we put out a call to other churches in the area and said, "Let's get our Christian communities together and coordinate our efforts." I believed that if we could keep our egos out of the way and work together, the *Church* in Katy—not merely the churches of Katy but the body of Christ in our community—could do something that would have eternal repercussions.

Within twenty-four hours, more than 150 pastors and ministry leaders responded to the call. We sketched out on a whiteboard the many needs and opportunities to work together and we determined who could provide what: everything from food, clothing, and transportation, to temporary housing and medical assistance. We also listed some things people would need in the weeks ahead. For instance, we knew hundreds of people would need coordinated efforts to tear out water-logged carpet and drywall from homes damaged by the floodwater. Others would need medical and financial help. As the relief efforts continued, I soon learned that the same type of teamwork was happening with churches all over the Houston area.

The churches of Houston plunged into the work, and I got to witness an incredible coordinated effort of Christians investing in their neighbors. I was grateful not only that Kingsland stepped up but also that we got to work so closely with our fellow community churches. There was a beautiful, mutual trust built on years of working side by side and relational investments among our leaders. We trusted one another, and that mattered immensely when the chips were down. I'll never forget a dear friend and pastor in our area approaching me after our meeting and saying simply, "We trust you. Just tell us what to do." He knew that our motives were pure, and because of that mutual trust, we were able to move at lightning speed.

We set up a blog and website tagged KatyDisaster Response.com, and our missions pastor, Omar Garcia, made it a resource where anyone in the city could find help and supplies. We did not brand anything we were doing with our Kingsland logo, and other churches did the same. The point was that our neighbors knew that we loved them because God loved them. Within three hours of Omar getting the site ready to outfit whatever needs people had, several staff members and I stopped by a shelter at Cinco Ranch High School. Outside the school was a person we didn't even know who was handing out cards with the website address on it. "Here's a place you can go if you need resources or to find help," he told people.

Sometimes the table is eminently practical: in desperate times, people may need food before they are ready to consider biblical truth or spiritual help. But in that physical and tangible help, something spiritual is at play. Jesus healed people—the blind man, the bleeding woman—before He preached to them. He met their physical needs. At other times, He combined both, feeding people spiritual truth as well as physical food, as He did when He fed five thousand people who had listened to Him teach all day.

Each church seemed to find its own niche in the massive relief effort that was underway. The Fellowship in Cinco Ranch established a huge warehouse with supplies for families. CrossRoad Church did the same on the north side. Several congregations coordinated cleanup efforts, others helped to find housing for displaced families, and still more helped to house churches who had lost their own buildings.

Besides mobilizing an army of people to help clean out homes, it seemed only fitting that Kingsland would do something on a large scale to restore not only the people of Houston but the tables as well: our biggest job was providing food to people all over the city. Our base of operation at Kingsland was a huge feeding center that we operated in partnership with the Red Cross and Southern Baptist Disaster Relief. Each day following the flood, we fed more than twenty thousand people in our church parking lot. That went on for weeks. It was an enormous effort and volunteers came from all over the country to help us. The heart of what we did revolved around providing meals. We were determined that nobody would have to go without food. If people couldn't come to us for a meal, we took a hot meal to them.

Many of the displaced people who had been evacuated were dropped off at schools and then transferred to other places that were serving as shelters. At Exley Elementary School, for example, National Guard amphibious vehicles brought in people who had been rescued from their homes, many of which were in areas where the water was more than six feet high. These people had nothing. They needed more than just a cot. They needed a family.

At Cinco Ranch High School, there were mounds of supplies that compassionate people brought in to help evacuees so people could "go shopping" for basic needs, and then they'd try to go find a corner or some spot in a hallway where their family could plop down.

Some evacuees were being transferred to other parts of Houston to find refuge in temporary shelters. As I looked at the large number of people crammed into the shelters, it grieved me. I did not want to see any of our local folks transferred to other parts of Houston. We would take care of them somehow.

Moreover, as I witnessed the bittersweet attitudes of the people huddled in the shelters, it was easy to sense a combination of gratitude that they had been rescued from the flood or had otherwise made it to safety, and the heartbreaking despair that their homes were inundated by filthy water and it would be many months before life would ever look the same.

I went on social media and asked the Kingsland community, "Friends, I'm here at Exley Elementary School and there are evacuated flood victims crowded into the school. I know it is a stretch, but if there are some families who can come right now, if you are willing and can help a family, please come to Exley Elementary School and pick up an evacuated family, and take them home with you. We don't have any idea how long they might be with you, but they need help right now."

At the time I made the plea, I had no idea how many people in Katy needed a refuge, a temporary respite from the driving rains and floodwaters, or how many people could help. Nevertheless, I told some of the evacuees, "There are some families who are coming and you can have a warm bed." Some of the fathers were skeptical, but the moms were quick to embrace the possibility of getting out of the shelter.

Within a half hour, the first people to show up at the school were a couple from Scotland who were living and working in Katy. The Scottish couple picked up a Chinese family and took them home with them. All day long, people pulled up to the school in the pouring rain and wrapped their arms around other families. They greeted people whom they had never before met, and knew nothing about, yet they hugged them and took them home. Everyone, it seemed, had tears in their eyes.

We opened our homes and shared our tables. More than two hundred cars showed up with people willing to take flood victims into their homes. We had more cars than we had people who needed help. So we set up a system to adopt a family and host them. We had so many people who volunteered that we emptied out the shelters within thirty-six hours and still had more volunteers willing to take flood victims into their homes. People went from strangers to friends overnight.

Some evacuees stayed with families from area churches for a week or two. Others stayed for several months. Some transferred to hotels once FEMA funds became available. Through it all, many permanent friendships were formed.

Many of our small groups and community groups dove into helping people in need. So often, we'd learn of a need or a family that needed help, and by the time we got the information to our disaster relief ministry, the need had already been met by one of our community groups.

It wasn't the government that took the responsibility; it was the church. People who had recreational boats turned them into rescue boats, motoring them through one flooded neighborhood after another and hauling people out of danger. We had numerous people who picked up strangers who had been brought out by boat after having to abandon their homes in the flood and took them into their homes, allowing them to stay as long as necessary. Many people struck up deep friendships as a result of some of these serendipitous relationships.

While many people haven't been through a traumatic event like Harvey, everyone has a friend who's going through trauma. Sometimes others' problems seem so big we don't know what to do or say. When that happens, we can simply invite that friend to our table. We can meet a physical need they have. That may be enough in the moment. Especially if what they're going through is too difficult to talk about yet, simply inviting that person into your home may be enough.

While the flood waters from Hurricane Harvey were still receding, Omar Garcia and some local pastors and I gathered together in our church parking lot. The Texas branch of the Southern Baptist Relief organization had set up camp there, so during a lull in the action, we were talking casually with one of their leaders.

He said, "Pastor, you do realize that we are not yet done in New Orleans, dealing with the aftermath of Katrina? This is going to be a fifty-year rebuilding and recovery process." The governor of Texas had suggested something similar. During an interview broadcast on national television, Governor Greg Abbott said, "This is going to be a massive cleanup process. People need to understand this is not going to be a short-term project.

This is going to be a multi-year project for Texas to dig out of this catastrophe."[56]

I didn't want to argue, and I certainly respected our experienced leaders' opinions. But I looked at Omar and said, "No offense, but this is not going to take fifty years."

Omar smiled. He agreed. We both knew that the Christians in the Greater Houston area would not only take an active role in feeding, clothing, and temporarily housing people displaced by the flood but would be busy tearing out carpet and drywall in homes that had been flooded. They would work long hours in the heat, clearing fallen trees and brush and shoveling mud out of living rooms. The family of God knows how to work, and the people of Kingsland run to people in need. Omar and I knew that no government agency could compare with relief efforts motivated by God's love.

Certainly, in the city of Houston some areas took months to recover. But the churches across the region unified, and today the city has largely recovered well despite all the homes that were flooded. The churches of the community came together in unprecedented ways, collectively providing relief efforts.

Our church continued long-term ministries to the people who had been affected by Hurricane Harvey. Kingsland initiated a series of six dinner meetings with the evacuees, gathering them together to share a meal and tell their stories, distributing gift cards, and giving them permission to grieve. These meals were deeply meaningful. Many of the members of our church who had lost their homes were much more accustomed to helping others rather than being on the receiving end of help. I recall speaking to a man whose family had experienced flooding in their home; they were remaining in the livable portion of the house and actually housing some of their neighbors. I asked how things were going, and he said they were all exhausted. He said his wife had been in line for hours that morning just trying to get some toilet paper at the grocery store (which was continually struggling to keep essentials in stock at the time). I asked him why he hadn't simply called the church, as we had received many essential supplies such as these to distribute to those in need after the storm. He said, "I saw that in your email to us, but I figured those items are for victims."

I said, "Guess what? You're one of those victims!"

These people were used to being servants, and now they were being served. We also provided resources and places where they could come for counseling and marriage mentorship. We asked them, "What are your top three needs?"

Sometimes the need was as simple as moving a washing machine. Other needs were more emotional, some were financial, others more complicated. Whatever the need, we moved to meet it.

Ironically, this group did not diminish over time. They actually became more committed to gathering together with each other, encouraging one another, gathering around the table and having meals together, sharing food and practical information. The group whimsically called themselves the High Water Recipients. We had no formal agenda, but at each meeting the group ate together and one of the families told their story, and people would laugh, cry, and share together. Some of the flood victims were not even sure they wanted to go back to their homes; their lives were so discombobulated.

But the flood victims kept coming back to the dinners to share a meal around the table and to share their stories with each other. There was one thing the group refused to do: they would not allow themselves to turn into a pity party.

Just as the Scripture teaches, the experiences you go through are not merely meant for you; you go through them so you can be of help to someone else. There is a great deal of truth to the saying, "Your hurt will be your ministry." And if you look for opportunities, much of that ministry can take place in your own home, right around your dining table as you share meals with others.

Moreover, God has given many of us a gift of hospitality, and as the Scripture implies, some of us have entertained angels and been unaware of it.

A few weeks after Harvey, Deb Manning, who formerly worked in our Special Needs Department, was wearing a Kingsland T-shirt in Wal-Mart. A burly, rough-looking man saw the shirt and approached her until he stood in front of her.

"Hey," he said gruffly, pointing at her shirt.

"Yes?" Deb asked, somewhat hesitantly.

"Your church," the man said. "Your church . . ." he repeated hoarsely as tears filled his eyes. "*Your church . . .*" the man could say nothing else.

Deb went from feeling slightly fearful to wrapping her arms around the man in a spontaneous act. The two strangers stood there hugging in Wal-Mart for a few moments before they emotionally released their embrace, wiped the tears from their eyes, and went on their ways.

Deb said, "I never did find out what our church had done for him, but apparently it meant something significant in that man's life."

You may never know what sort of harvest the seeds of your selfless influence might bring. Only heaven will reveal the fruit of your efforts when you hear Jesus say, "Well done, good and faithful servant." But how incredible will it be when you are in heaven someday and somebody comes up to you and says, "Hey! Because you shared your table with me, you helped me to get here!"

When the Table Brings Hope from the Storm

Even during crisis, J. P. and Jessie saw the table as a respite. They focused their family around meaningful mealtimes for themselves and for others. Jessie is a great cook; she especially loves to bake, and she and J. P. are quite intentional about how they raise their children, creating special moments around the table. That has helped to sustain their family through the difficulties, and together they learned to hang on to God through the storm and the aftermath.

On the one-year anniversary of Hurricane Harvey, and every year since, the Pruitt family has initiated a celebration of the ways that God took care of them through the hurricane. They gather around the table and share a special dinner and dessert, and then they go upstairs to reminisce with the kids. "What are some of the cool ways that God took care of us?" J. P. asks their boys, Payton and Parker, and their daughter, Paisley. On that first anniversary when the memories were still fresh and raw, Payton remembered J. P.'s prayer almost verbatim, that God could work a miracle, and they would trust Him no matter what. The table at the Pruitt home will never be the same.

CHAPTER 12

The Table Outlives You

Omar Garcia has shared meals around tables in fifty countries. (He was with me on the journey to Somaliland I talked about at the beginning of the book.) As Kingsland's missions pastor, Omar is a modern-day pioneer, taking the gospel to people who have never before heard the message and to some who may even be antagonistic to hearing about Jesus. In 2023, Omar fulfilled a decades-old dream by walking across the entire nation of Bangladesh, praying all the way, and stopping throughout each day on the long journey to share meals and conversations with the people he met. The 316-kilometer trek took more than two weeks and placed him in front of hundreds of people, one table at a time. Along the way, in this spiritually hungry nation, fifty-seven people placed their faith in Jesus thanks to Omar's efforts.

I recently asked him, "Omar, is there any mission project we have ever done in which food or meals have not played integral parts?"

Omar was quick to reply, "Oh, no. Everywhere we take the gospel, food is a part of it. Especially in countries that are not friendly to the gospel message, if we can find a man of peace and have a meal in his home, we have a remarkable inroad into the community. In any outreach and every mission project, food has played an integral role in connecting people and building interpersonal bridges."

Omar is never bashful about inviting people to his table; nor is he reluctant to sit down around someone else's table, even in foreign lands, and he has seen firsthand, again and again, the power of the table and the way God uses food to change lives.

Omar and I were together recently in Bangladesh, meeting with a number of church leaders who were interested in the work we're doing with families in the United States. In Bangladesh, meals are usually served with no silverware, and those eating simply use their hands as a scoop for the rice-based entrees. The food was delicious, but I have to admit, it took some effort for me to get over the idea that I was doing something that would have been considered poor etiquette around my table growing up. Even so, there was something profoundly human and normal about delivering food literally from hand to mouth.

One of our meals was in an unair-conditioned room on a scorching-hot day with fourteen faithful pastors from Dhaka. These men had literally given up everything they owned and had risked their lives to follow Jesus in a culture with immense pressure to believe a different way. Theirs was a hard life, but there was a joy among these men that I've seldom witnessed in my lifetime. They recognized not only the One who had provided this special meal but also the blessing of walking with a God who loved them enough to send His only Son so they might have eternal life and join Him at the marriage supper of the Lamb.[57]

Restore the Table, Change the World

Just as your past tables have had an influence on you, the five meaningful mealtimes will have a significant effect on your family's future—sometimes in ways that you may not discover until much later.

Part of our DNA at Kingsland is to "go beyond," to go where the need is and where most other people don't have the interest or the ability to go. We do this not merely from humanitarian motives but because we have a mandate. Jesus commanded His followers to go into all the world sharing His message of good news and making disciples, baptizing, and teaching people how to follow Him. Taking and presenting the gospel to the entire world often seems so unrealistic, so ethereal that some people get the impression we are talking about taking a journey into outer space, the final frontier, someplace scary, or to the wildest jungles of Africa—and that may happen for some people. But for most of us, "going into all the world" means that you are going to get together, to make connections with real people, and often that begins around a table.

Rarely as adults do we forge new relationships without food or some sort of meal. In fact, I'm not sure any single event has been more important when we've traveled into largely Muslim areas than the sharing of meals. Many Middle Eastern cultures are well known for their hospitality to strangers despite their religious differences. Sitting down for a meal together breaks down barriers in a way that nothing else does.

A Table Full of Stories

When you commit to having five meaningful mealtimes each week with the people you love, unusual things may happen naturally among your family members. Creative ideas may occur spontaneously, new adventures may seem suddenly possible, and many other transformational conversations may take place. Plans, goals, events, and attitudes that flow out of those times around the table might make history and change the course of people's lives. Your five meaningful mealtimes may impact people that you have never even met or may never personally meet, but the influence of those five regular meals may expand exponentially for years to come.

I first met Steve Hyde, who directs a missions program in Cambodia, over a meal at the kitchen table in the home of Dave and Kara Potts, members of our Kingsland congregation. Kara and Dave live and breathe missions, and Kara has been to Cambodia on several missions and service trips. They wanted me to meet Steve so I could get a better understanding of his work in Southeast Asia.

Along with Omar Garcia, Lana and I sat around the Potts' kitchen table eating pizza with Kara and Dave; their daughter, Avery; their sons, Cooper and Carson; and Steve and his wife, Noit, from Cambodia. The Hydes told us Noit's story about surviving the Cambodian killing fields as a young woman. Steve was a missionary kid whose dad had gotten killed in the Philippines. Yet God chose to use two wounded people. As a young man, Steve committed his life to Christ, and his life had totally changed. Today, he and Noit are back in Cambodia helping others to discover a relationship with Jesus. They have a church and school there as well as a facility for training pastors.

Talking with Steve and Noit Hyde about their work in Cambodia, I sensed that God was up to something, that there were things happening at the table that evening that were much bigger than us. Something historic was happening, something earth-shaking. God was opening our hearts and minds to get a fresh vision of the need and potential ministry in Cambodia.

I realized that this pizza dinner was a divine opportunity, an encounter that could change future generations because Kara and Dave and their family members are so intentional about representing Jesus and seeing lives transformed. They have exposed all of their kids to missions opportunities since birth, and Cooper, especially, a naturally vibrant leader, grew up with an awareness that the world was much bigger than his hometown, and the needs were much greater. I could not possibly have imagined that night just how far-reaching the conversation around the table would turn out to be.

Cooper and his dad were tightly bonded, but Dave traveled quite often for his business, so Kara and Cooper—both early risers—became "breakfast buddies." They established the habit of getting up early and having breakfast together as often as possible. During those breakfasts, the conversation often turned to various needs that exist among people in impoverished areas around the world. Unquestionably, those breakfasts with Cooper and Kara contributed to Cooper's understanding of the world beyond his home and his passion to help people who are hurting.

Cooper was active at Kingsland, helping kids in our Vacation Bible School, serving on weekends in numerous inner-city Houston outreach projects with his parents, and working in our "Caring for Katy" effort each year along with other members of the Kingsland student groups. Cooper looked forward to going on his senior trip to Israel with fellow graduates.

In September 2018, Cooper and some of his buddies went to Wemberley, in the Texas Hill Country, for a day to ride all-terrain vehicles. They were having a great time, but then somehow they rolled the ATV into a lake. Apparently, the accident knocked Cooper unconscious underwater and his friends couldn't find him. One of the friends ran to a nearby house, and the adults there called for help. But by the time the paramedics arrived and were able to locate Cooper, he had been underwater for more than fifteen minutes.

Cooper's untimely death crushed the hearts of many in our community. It seemed to make no sense. We all wrestled with questions of how this could happen and why God would allow such a tragedy to take place in the life of a young man who had so much potential to change his world for the better.

Yet we knew that Cooper was with Jesus and we believed that God would bring good from what the Enemy had intended for evil.

At Cooper's memorial services, with overflow crowds at Kingsland as well as in Cooper's high school, God showed up in both challenging and comforting ways, challenging people to be brokenhearted over the things that concerned Cooper and comforting people with an assurance that Cooper's life and influence would far outlive him.

Then a beautiful thing began to happen. After Cooper's tragic death, people wanted to respond, to do something to honor Cooper and express love for the things he loved. Large amounts of money poured in, donated by friends and raised by various groups to support causes dear to the Potts family. The family established the Cooper Potts Memorial Fund to oversee and distribute those funds to people in need.

The junior class at the public high school in Katy raised more than $10,000 for the Cooper Potts Memorial Fund. I met with a number of the public school officials and the students—many of whom were wearing "Live Like Coop" shirts. I did my best to explain to them the background for Cooper's passion and how their heartfelt donations would be used. "There is a less than fifty percent literacy rate for women in Nepal, so we are building an education center there, and you are helping to do that," I shared with them.

Another need, and a natural and obvious place that had been in Cooper's heart, was that of the Hydes'

ministry in Cambodia. At the time of Cooper's accident, Steve Hyde had a new school under construction
in Cambodia. Through donations to the Cooper Potts
Memorial Fund, Steve said, "We're going to name the
new school after Cooper Potts." Partly funded by Vacation Bible School offerings at Kingsland, we were also
able to build an additional wing for the school.

Today, there are Cooper Potts educational initiatives in Guatemala, a school in Nepal, and a school in
Uganda. These educational facilities influence kids who
would otherwise not be going to school, but thanks to the
love and compassion stirred by Cooper Potts, about five
hundred kids are getting an education and learning what
it means to have a relationship with Jesus Christ.

Cooper and his mom probably shared at least five
hundred breakfasts. Only heaven will reveal how many
lives have been changed positively thanks to the conversations and spiritual transactions that took place at that
breakfast table. Something happened at that table that
changed the world for better.

For years to come, there will be generations of kids
in Nepal, Cambodia, and Uganda whose lives will be
influenced because Cooper and Kara ate breakfast each
morning and talked about the needs in our world.

What began at the breakfast table continues to have
a positive, eternal influence that will far outlive not only
Cooper but his entire family. Hopefully, there will be

people in heaven because Cooper and his mom shared five meaningful meals together each week.

Today in Cambodia, we continue to use food as a major part of our work there, with team members sharing a meal with people in every village where we hope to minister. For instance, we host one seminar for approximately two hundred women to talk about best practices in caring for their families physically and spiritually, simple ideas that they can incorporate in their homes. The seminar is always conducted around round tables, with people working together and eating together. We don't set up rows. The women do everything together; everything is around the table.

We do something similar with the kids in Cambodia, providing meals and encouraging them to trust in God for a great future. We make it a point to listen to the kids. Some have families that couldn't afford them, so they literally gave up on raising them. We let the kids know that they are special and that they matter to their heavenly Father. A lot of those intimate conversations take place around the table where there are fewer barriers to communication.

What's on the menu? It's Southeast Asia, so we have rice and some sort of protein, usually chicken or fish. We also try to give the kids something they wouldn't normally get, including fun drinks and snacks, and we also attempt to do healthy meals if possible. Many of these nutritious meals for kids are financed by the Cooper Potts Memorial Fund.

Cooper's reputation as a kid who loved people who are hurting has outlived him. It is truly remarkable for a sixteen-year-old to have that kind of influence, but kids who knew Cooper respected him and knew that Cooper cared about the nations. That's why the students picked up on his passion. He was a hero to the underdog or the marginalized kid. He was a quiet individual, but his peers respected him.

Cooper Potts lived with no regrets. His family feels the same way. They loved every moment of Cooper's life, and certainly grieve his loss, but they live confidently with the hope that they will see Cooper again in heaven. They understand that his life has made a positive difference in this world, and continues to do so, as the outpouring of concern continues to this day. They also understand that a short life need not be an insignificant life.

Are five meaningful mealtimes each week together with the people you love really all that significant? They are to Dave and Kara Potts and their family. And they are to the many people's lives influenced by their compassion.

*　*　*　*　*

Let's think about your table. What will it take for you to reclaim your own table, to "own" it and establish five meaningful mealtimes with the ones you love? What legacy of time around your table might God redeem and restore? With whom can you share meaningful mealtimes around your table? What does it mean for you to invite people to your table? And what about your five meaningful mealtimes will impact generations to come?

All of that and more can happen as you diligently establish and maintain five meaningful mealtimes each week with the people you love.

As your family table changes, invite somebody to join you for meals. You may just change their world. Reach out to someone else's family. Or go and join someone else at their table in some part of the world and help change their future forever.

You can do this! It matters to you, and you can be sure that God will help you to restore the table and establish a habit of having five meaningful mealtimes each week. As it becomes a part of your life, why not invite someone outside of your circle to join you? You can be sure that you and your family will be changed for the better.

It's not an exaggeration to say that the mealtimes in my life have shaped and defined me. I'd be willing to bet the same is true for you. Moreover, I'm convinced the power of the table will increase in the days and years ahead. We're living in times of tremendous uncertainty. Many believe that society is facing almost insurmountable challenges. Will the family survive another generation? Do we have an imminent war on the horizon between conflicted nations or ideologies? What about the changing landscape of faith and church involvement? Is there any hope for the days ahead?

You can call me a naive optimist, but I will unabashedly say *yes*. The very best days are ahead. And what if all of these complex issues share, at least in part, one timeless solution? What if the answers lie in a habit that's been right in front of us all along?

Will having five meaningful mealtimes each week make a difference in your life and the lives of your family members? In the lives of others in your community? In your world?

Count on it.

The Scripture offers us a glorious invitation: "Taste and see that the LORD is good."[58]

CONVERSATION STARTERS FOR THE TABLE

(Adapted from Pastor Brad Flurry,
EmpoweredHomes.org)

When are you (or when have you been) most afraid?
What has been the happiest day of your life?
If you could change one thing in the world, what would
　you change?
If you could change one thing about yourself, what
　would you change?
What does "being in love" mean?
What is the most important thing in your life?
What is the one thing you couldn't live without?
What is your favorite movie of all time? Why?
What is your favorite book of all time? Why?
What cartoon character would you most like to be?
What is the hardest thing about being ____ years old?
What is the best thing about being ____ years old?

Describe your perfect day.

What job would you never want to have?

Who is your best friend? Why is that person your best friend?

What's your favorite car and why?

Who would you most like to meet?

In what other country would you most like to live?

What things don't boys understand about girls?

What things don't girls understand about boys?

Why do you think people use curse words?

When was the last time you cried? What did you cry about?

How are you feeling about the next school year?

What's the hardest part about going to school?

What should parents do when their children don't obey?

If you could have any animal as a pet, which would you choose?

What embarrasses you the most?

If you could take a family vacation any place in the world, where would you go?

Do you think it's more important to be rich or kind?

If you had three wishes, what would they be? (You're not allowed to wish for money or another wish!)

Do you know how much your family loves you? How can you tell?

What is your greatest ambition in life?

What brings you the greatest joy in your life?

(Pastor Brad is the executive pastor of ministries at Kingsland Baptist Church in Katy, Texas. The amazing story of how God redeemed his family table appears in chapter 6 of this book.)

ENDNOTES

1. Cody C. Delistraty, "The Importance of Eating Together," *The Atlantic,* July 18, 2014, https://www.theatlantic .com/health/archive/2014/07/the-importance-of-eating -together/374256/.

2. Wonjeong Chae et al., "Association between Eating Behaviour and Diet Quality: Eating Alone vs. Eating with Others," *Nutrition Journal* 17, no. 117 (December 2018), https://doi.org/10.1186/s12937-018-0424-0.

3. Juana Summers, Vincent Acovino, and Christopher Intagliata, "America Has a Loneliness Epidemic. Here Are 6 Steps to Address It," recording, *All Things Considered,* NPR, May 2, 2023, https://www.npr.org/2023 /05/02/1173418268/loneliness-connection-mental-health -dementia-surgeon-general.

4. B. S. Bowden and J. M. Zeisz, "Supper's on! Adolescent adjustment and frequency of family mealtimes," (paper presented at the 105th Annual Meeting of the American Psychological Association, Chicago, Illinois, August 1997).

5. Shira Offer. "Assessing the Relationship between Family Mealtime Communication and Adolescent Emotional Well-Being Using the Experience Sampling Method,"

Journal of Adolescence 36, no. 3 (June 2013): 577–85, https://doi.org/10.1016/j.adolescence.2013.03.007.

6. Shira Offer, "Assessing the Relationship between Family Mealtime Communication and Adolescent Emotional Well-being Using the Experience Sampling Method," *Journal of Adolescence* 36, no. 3 (April 2013): 577–85, https://doi.org/10.1016/j.adolescence.2013.03.007.

7. Chris Westfall, "Leadership Development Is a $366 Billion Industry: Here's Why Most Programs Don't Work," *Forbes*, June 20, 2019, https://www.forbes.com/sites /chriswestfall/2019/06/20/leadership-development-why -most-programs-dont-work/?sh=ac585b961de4.

8. Luke 19:5 NASB.

9. Matthew 9:9–13.

10. Luke 24:13–35.

11. John 21:1–23.

12. Revelation 19:7–16.

13. Matthew 4:4 NASB, quoting Deuteronomy 8:3.

14. Acts 2:46–47 ESV.

15. John Bowlby, "The Nature of the Child's Tie to His Mother," chap. 14 in Andrew C. Furman and Steven T. Levy (eds.), *Influential Papers from the 1950s*, 1st ed. (Boca Raton, FL: Routledge, 2003), 222–273, https://doi .org/10.4324/9780429475931-15.

16. Alyson Rees, Sally Holland, and Andrew Pithouse, "Food in Foster Families: Care, Communication and Conflict," *Children & Society* 26, no. 2 (March 2012): 100–111, https://doi.org/10.1111/j.1099-0860.2010.00332.x.

17. See Genesis 3:1–6.

18. Deuteronomy 6:4–9 NASB 1995.

19. Abigail Carroll, *Three Squares: The Invention of the American Meal* (New York: Basic Books, 2013), xvi.

20. Delistraty, "Eating Together."

21. Carroll, *Three Squares*, 16.

22. Mackensie Griffin, "'No Place for Discontent': A History of the Family Dinner in America," The Salt, NPR, February 16, 2016, https://www.npr.org/sections/thesalt/2016/02/16/459693979/no-place-for-discontent-a-history-of-the-family-dinner-in-america.

23. Carroll, *Three Squares*, 67.

24. Carroll, *Three Squares*, 67.

25. J. Flanders, *The Making of Home: The 500-Year Story of How Our Houses Became Our Homes* (New York: Thomas Dunne Books, 2015).

26. "Chicken Doritos Casserole," Jam Hands, updated March 7, 2023, adapted from Deanna, "Mexican Chicken Casserole" on Domestic Chicky, http://www.jamhands.net/2011/05/mexican-chicken-casserole.html.

27. James Clear, *Atomic Habits*, 1st ed. (NY: Avery, 2018).

28. W. Bradford Wilcox, et al., *Do Two Parents Matter More Than Ever?*, The American Enterprise Institute September 20, 2023, https://www.aei.org/articles/do-two-parents-matter-more-than-ever/

29. 1 Timothy 4:7 CSB.

30. Ephesians 4:20 CSB.

31. Ephesians 4:24 CSB.

32. 2 Peter 1:3 CSB.

33. 2 Peter 1:4 CSB.

34. Ephesians 4:22–24 CSB.

35. Exodus 20:2 NASB.

36. Ephesians 5:1–2 NASB.

37. John 14:1–2 CSB.

38. John 14:5 CSB.

39. John 14:6 CSB.

40. K. A. Lee et al., "A 50-Year Prospective Study of the Psychological Sequelae of World War II Combat," *American Journal of Psychiatry* 152, no. 4 (1995): 516–22.

41. John Trent, June 11, 2020, interview by the author, Franklin, TN.

42. John Trent, June 11, 2020, interview by the author, Franklin, TN.

43. See Luke 5:1–11.

44. Malachi 2:16 NASB.

45. See Matthew 19:8–9.

46. Nikki Lee, "Easy Chicken Pot Pie," Soulfully Made, October 4, 2017, https://www.soulfullymade.com/easy-chicken-pot-pie/.

47. Mark 2:27 ESV.

48. Revelation 3:20 CSB.

49. William Butler Yeats, "Fairy and Folk Tales of the Irish Peasantry," Project Gutenberg, accessed August 21, 2023, https://www.gutenberg.org/files/33887/33887-h/33887-h.htm#Page_84.

50. Ephesians 5:1–2 CSB.

51. Genesis 27:34 CSB.

52. Genesis 1:27 CSB.

53. Gary Smalley and John Trent, *The Blessing* (Nashville, TN: Thomas Nelson, 1986), 24.

54. Proverbs 11:25 ESV.

55. Chris Huber, "2017 Hurricane Harvey: Facts, FAQs, and How to Help," World Vision, accessed July 8, 2020, https://www.worldvision.org/disaster-relief-news-stories /2017-hurricane-harvey-facts#death-toll.

56. Morgan Winsor and Julia Jacobo, "Parts of Texas Still Face 'Ongoing Threat' of Flooding, Governor Says," ABC News, September 1, 2017, https://abcnews.go.com /US/hurricane-harvey-recovery-multi-year-project-texas -governor/story?id=49560131.

57. Revelation 19.

58. Psalm 34:8 CSB.

100% of the profits from this book will go to
hunger-related initiatives throughout the world.
We pray that this allows families to enjoy the
blessing of mealtimes who otherwise would not.